52 NEW FRIENDS ™

ERICA MCBETH

www.ericamcbeth.com

Cover design by Bily Foster

This book is dedicated to

Owen Brown

Once, I made a promise to a super fan to include his name as one of the characters in my next book. Little did I know that the characters in the next book would be real-life characters so the opportunity wasn't there.

I hope this will suffice.

In loving memory of

Austin Hansen

The Premise of 52 New Friends

Last fall I had a revelation. Something wonderful happened to me…and I had no one to share it with.

I am a forty-two-year old, divorced, childless woman with a family that has done a very good job at alienating themselves from me. If life were a big, patchwork quilt, I feel like my portion is a single, solitary patch that has been left on the floor and forgotten.

And in quiet moments, I am lonely.

I'm embarrassed to admit it but sometimes, I even feel sorry for myself. Silence gives you plenty of time to pick apart all your flaws.

Over the past two years, I've done a lot of online dating but frankly, I think the over-forty-and-single category needs more therapy than they do dates. I'll even include myself in that observation.

And then, a few weeks ago, I went to a charity walk for suicide prevention. I told myself I was there to support other people but as I stood in the crowd of nearly two thousand people who had gathered, I realized there are people who leave this world because they, too, pick apart their flaws in silence and in isolation…and little do they realize how much they are missed. Maybe this world needs fewer meaningless dates and more real connections. And maybe that needs to start with me.

So, for 2018, I have made a goal of developing 52 new connections in my life. I will call them friends. In this social experiment, I am hoping I can meet interesting people who may be different from me. My intention is to listen and maybe enrich their life in some way, although, I would be open and grateful if they enriched mine. And I'm going to blog about it each week which frankly, is a little unnerving. I'm a planner and I have no idea where this is going to go. But life is an adventure. And so it begins…

The Beginning

Friend #1 - Melissa

First of all, I am overwhelmed by the outpouring of support for this endeavor.

Last Wednesday night, I asked my Facebook friends for referrals of people I might not already know. I figured this was a safe way to meet new friends but frankly, I wasn't sure how it would go. Apparently, I struck a chord. As of today, my blog has had almost 500 pageviews with numerous friends approaching me about potential friend referrals.

One of those was a gentleman named Kurt. Kurt and I were part of a network marketing company almost ten years ago. Every now and then I will see something from him pop up in my Facebook feed but he is one of those friends who would have probably disappeared into obscurity if it wasn't for social media.

He said: "I have a friend named Melissa who would love to make a new friend." So I messaged Melissa. Neither of us was working on Friday afternoon so I suggested we grab some coffee.

Now I know what you are thinking: It isn't 2018 YET! But does change really need to start on a certain day? Why can't you just start it right away? So we did.

I was sitting outside of the coffee shop when I saw Melissa coming towards me. My first impression was that she was bubbly with long, loose dark curly hair and she was wearing the coolest pair of blue eyeglasses I've ever seen. No surprise - she works for an optician – but if I had glasses, I'd want some just like Melissa's.

We started chatting and I kept looking at her in those blue eyeglasses. I didn't want to come out and say it but there was something about the way Kurt had said she "would love to make a new friend" that suggested tragedy. So I started asking questions and fishing for that invisible thing…and Melissa told me in August she had gone through a bad breakup. Melissa said one moment she and her boyfriend were talking about getting married and the next moment they were broken up. I could tell by the way she said it that the memory was still painful.

But she was not defeated. Melissa also said that ten years ago she had been diagnosed with a thyroid condition. For those of you who know about such things, I am sorry I do not remember the specific name of the condition, but Melissa told me ten years ago she had gained a large amount of weight in one year for no particular reason. She said she had been keeping the condition at bay with medication but had recently been working with a nutritionist, who is also a physician, to adjust her diet to get rid of the illness. Melissa said she believes these dietary changes can put her thyroid condition into remission. She's been doing a lot of research. And in her sassy blue spectacles, I believed her. I have a feeling Melissa is very good at research.

We'd been chatting for over an hour so the last question I asked her was: "What one thing would you like to be remembered for?"

She thought about it for a moment and then reluctantly said there were two things. We never got around to the second thing because the first thing she would like to be remembered for is: "Don't judge a book by its cover."

And immediately my mind flashed back to earlier in the conversation when we were talking about Melissa's breakup. She said she thought the reason her boyfriend broke up with her was because she didn't fit the image he wanted.

In any normal social situation, I would have brushed over that remark, afraid to call out the elephant in the room. But this was two strangers meeting for the first time in a coffee shop. Knowing that, I felt emboldened. So I asked... "Is it because of your weight?"

And two perfectly formed teardrops appeared in Melissa's eyes. She took off her glasses and said... "yes".

And my heart just broke.

The value of a person is not measured by a number on a scale. That's reality as it should be. Being a woman, I know all too well the societal pressures to stay thin. It's why I run even though I hate it. It's why I feel guilty for having a donut at work, but I don't personally know the pain of how society acts when someone is considered "heavy". I've heard that people say mean things, which must be a dagger to a woman's self-worth each and every time they are uttered. And I marveled at the bravery of Melissa's admission. How many women are out there who keep themselves locked away and alone because they think the world is going to reject them for what they look like?

I reached out and touched Melissa's arm. I looked her in her eyes and I said, "You are perfect just the way you are." And she is! When I look at Melissa, I don't see weight. I see a girl you'd want to split a bottle of wine with on a Friday night because you know at the end of the evening you'd be rolling around on the carpet in a fit of giggles. And maybe, as a community, we should say those things more often…because they are the truth.

I feel blessed to have connected with this girl. And I can only hope that Melissa's vulnerability might reach and inspire someone else out there who has closed themselves off from the world. The truth is…You are worthy. And more importantly, you are not alone.

The World Traveler

Friend #2 - Erica

A group of American tourists in Bulgaria decided to plan a day trip. There were three destinations on their agenda but as they were looking at the map, they realized these locations were slightly farther apart than they had, at first, realized. This meant the trip might require more daylight hours than fell in a single day. They heard there was a lodge on the top of a mountain at the final destination but it worked on first-come-first-serve accommodations, which meant they may or may not be able to stay the night. Deciding that it was worth taking the chance, Erica and a few of her friends packed small overnight bags, preparedness for the possibility of what was to come.

The day wore on and after two stops, the group finally parked below the huge mountain, home to their final destination. They asked the parking lot attendant in broken Bulgarian if she knew if the lodge at the top of the mountain was full for the night. She indicated that she did not know. The hikers then asked if the rental cars would be safe for the night if they decided to stay. The Bulgarian woman said she thought so, the words coming out in broken English. Erica decided the woman was not much help, after all. Nevertheless, the group carried on.

Two-by-two they took chairlifts to reach the start of the trail. Just as they were loading, they noticed the clouds shift and a fog overtook them as they rose through the air. At one point, the fog was so thick they could not see the chair in front of them. Erica looked at her watch. It was 4:30. The lift closed at 6:30. The hike was three hours. She worried if the lodge was full, they would not have time to finish and get back to the lift before it closed for the night. She looked at her cell phone. The battery was almost dead. Then, Erica and her seatmate noticed two familiar faces floating down in the opposite direction. A few people had broken off from the group earlier in the day, deciding to skip the monastery and go straight to the hike above. Erica waved to them, and they yelled that two others were still on the hike. After a thumbs-up, the pair disappeared back through the fog and the chairlift crept steadily up the mountain.

Erica's group was deposited in a clearing. The mysterious lodge hovered nearby. Exiting the trailhead, Erica saw the two missing members of their group. They smiled. The women hugged. The men shook hands. Everyone was full of tales of their adventures from the day. Together, they all went to make inquiries at the lodge, whose architecture was of the traditional Bulgarian style. It was unique to foreigners and such that has rarely been seen in American photographs since the area has only recently lost the daunting stigma of Communism and opened itself back up to tourism. Because the lodge, itself, was so magnificent and upon hearing that sleeping arrangements could be made for everyone, the entire group made the decision to stay including the pair who had just finished their hike, who had not thought to pack an overnight bag.

That night was filled with laughter as the group of American tourists gathered around the crackling fire in the main room, listening to the stories of some of the local Bulgarians, who were also staying at the lodge. They drank the local wine. They dined on local cuisine. Erica said it was the most fun she's ever had.

And just like her trip to the mountain, with a little preparedness, Erica has managed to maneuver through uncertain times and live, what many would consider, an adventurous life. And that was never more evident than when she sauntered into the coffee shop to meet me, fresh from yoga, with her hair tied up in a messy bun. She greeted me and asked, "So what's this all about?"

A mutual friend had facilitated the match up via social media with apparently, little explanation on either side. We were just two girls, meeting up, unsure of where the meeting would lead. I immediately liked Erica's openness to whatever the world brings. We are alike in that respect.

Where we are not alike, is that Erica has traveled all over the world. I asked how she was first bit by the travel bug and she said she met a couple of Brits while attending a friend's wedding right around the end of her college term. These gentlemen were on their gap year, which is a time period between university and the beginning of one's career that young adults use to travel around the world. The Brits told her stories about backpacking through India and Thailand. At the time, Erica didn't even realize those were places one could visit for fun…and she was fascinated.

She told a friend from work that she wanted to take a gap year. Of course, she said it as she was trying to work out the details in her head. She confided to this friend that she was thinking of working a year and then taking her gap year immediately after. Her friend shook her head and said, "Why don't you just go now? If you don't go now, other things will come up and you will never go." And Erica knew she was right. So she thought about it more, really dove into the finances of such a trip and realized she had enough money saved to live abroad for three months. The following day, she excitedly told her friend of her plans while they were at work and as they conspired, Erica's boss happened to walk by. "Does this mean you're quitting?" he asked. It wasn't until later that night Erica realized she had actually just quit her job.

It wasn't that she was without fear but the more people Erica told about her trip, the more real it became. Every person that knew propelled her to take the next step and before she knew it, she was spending three months traveling through Western Europe, Eastern Europe and Asia. On her way back, she had her choice between a layover in Sydney or Hong Kong. She chose Sydney, Australia because, well, that's another continent she'd never visited. And if she was going to have an eight-hour layover anyway, she might as well stay the night there. And if she was going to spend the night, she might as well stay a couple of days. Apparently, one adventure begets another. And then that becomes the new normal.

Erica did come back to Phoenix. She found a job she loved with co-workers she considered like family. And then one day, after many years, her beloved company was sold…and the layoffs were fierce. As a graphic designer, Erica knew that freelancing was a possibility but that meant losing the stability she'd built, the steady paycheck. She worried her income would take a hit and she mourned because life, as she knew it, was now over.

This isn't a woman who is superhuman. She has cried. She's had heartbreak. She has been afraid. The difference is she feels the emotions, accepts where she is and like moving up that fog encased mountain in Bulgaria, she finds a way. Sometimes that way leads her into more adventure. After Erica lost her job, she found a way to work as a freelancer and once again, travel the world. And sometimes Erica's way leads her back home. Right now, she focused on home improvement and is developing thicker roots in her community. Hers is a life that hasn't been crafted with cookie cutter expectations but one that has been created with a little preparedness, a will to find her way and a sense of adventure that takes her wherever the wind blows.

The Country Boy

Friend #3 – Rodney

Most people don't realize it but there are two types of people in this world: city folk and country folk. Because most of those reading this will be city folk, let me explain the difference.

When someone is born into a country life, their life is simple. Nothing important is ever rushed and often silence is the most beautiful voice. They understand the importance of stopping to watch a sunset. The people they trust are the ones they sat next to in grade school, kissed under the school bleachers and sang with in the church choir. They trust those from the same root and they often wonder, "How can life get any better than this?" It is an idealistic life. They love and they die with a blessed innocence of violence. And they see city folk as chaotic, unbalanced and misinformed on all the ways life should be.

This story is about a country boy named Rodney, who found himself displaced.

Rodney spent his childhood on a farm in Iowa, buried deep in the heart of this country. He has two older brothers and an older sister. There was also once a younger brother who passed away when Rodney was six-years-old, a brother that has been gone nearly fifty years but still significant enough to mention. When Rodney speaks of Iowa, the edges of mouth involuntarily tilt upward and the crinkles around his eyes relax. For Rodney, Iowa is a deep, long breath.

He moved to Phoenix when he was nineteen years old and for the longest time, just kept trying to get back there. It's not just the land. It's the memories, the people. It's a part of his soul. He never married and says he regrets spending too much time on the wrong women. He says it like he had a choice…but in my mind, that's the purest definition of a country boy.

 The media likes to portray country folks as ignorant rednecks because that's what they think people want to see. That's what gets ratings, but when country folk find a person they care about enough to want to spend the rest of their life with, there aren't any additional questions to ask. Commitment to God, country and family runs iron-clad and deep. Because the women Rodney chose were likely city girls, they probably didn't understand the nature of his commitment to them, the simplicity of just loving someone because you do.

"I just wish I could just get a woman to listen to me but sometimes, it's hard to get a word in edgewise," he said. I laughed because let's face it, sometimes, as women, we are full of a bunch of clatter. A country man's thought process is slower, which has nothing to do intelligence. Forming the right words is difficult. Being is easy.

And there is one place that always brings Rodney joy. He's been a lifelong motorcycle rider since he crashed his older brother's new Honda into a barn when everyone thought he was too young to ride. For most of his life, he's had a motorcycle obsession. It's where he feels most alive. It's the way the seat of his Harley kicks his legs and hips out for personal comfort, the unremitting rumble of the motor. It's the air's movement that envelopes him like an acceptance on the road. Riding, for Rodney, is like running on angel wings. As an experienced rider, he knows every part of his bike, understands every movement and every contour of the road. It's bliss, a small piece of heaven on earth.

Of course, if Rodney told this story, it would be very different. Like most men, he sees the world with less romantic imagery and more hard specifics. In a sense, this is the tale of a man that has been translated through the eyes of a woman. I chose to tell it this way because underneath Rodney's grit is an unmistakable purity that is less about words and more about the person he truly is.

In A Rut

Friend #4 – Chacara

Last fall, one of my car's headlights burned out. I know next to nothing about cars, but a burned-out headlight seemed like a stupid thing to take to my mechanic to fix. I change burned out light bulbs at my condo all the time. So really… how hard can it be?

I bought a new headlight at my local auto parts store and watched three YouTube videos on the topic. I put on a dirty wife-beater tank and some old jeans, popped the hood of my car and proceeded to dismantle the headlight like it was the most natural thing in the world. I did pretty well until I got to the pin that held the bulb in place. Each of the YouTube videos I watched said dismantling the pin was the hardest part and none of them really seemed to capture exactly how to get it out. I struggled with that pin for what seemed like ten minutes. I was starting to get frustrated. My thumb and my pointer fingers developing welts, and then a friendly voice behind me said, "Are you trying to change out the headlight?"

I turned to see a friendly woman I'd smiled at a dozen times who lived in my condo complex. "Yes," I grunted. "But I'm not doing very well. There's this pin that is the devil to get out."

"I just changed out mine last week," she said. "Would you like me to help you?"

My jaw loosened and eyebrows knitted together in what probably looked like a Basset Hound face. "Yes," I said, a little closer to tears than I would have liked.

The woman knew exactly what she was doing. Old cars and necessity had made her rather handy under the hood. She pulled that pesky pin and together, we installed a new bulb. Afterwards, I hugged her, thanked her and assured her I couldn't have done it without her.

And that's how I met Chacara.

Months passed. There had been no chance meeting with Chacara since the incident with my headlight, but I'd thought about her every time I went to get into my car. She could have simply walked by me that afternoon with my upper body bent under the hood …but she hadn't. And I was grateful. Very few people offer to help without expectation and I wanted to return the kindness. Last week, as I was pulling my car into my parking spot, Chacara was locking the door to her condo on the way to pick up her niece. I flagged her down, told her about my friend experiment and we agreed to meet up for coffee on a Saturday morning.

Chacara has three children ages thirteen, nine and two. I'm always hesitant to steal away from a mother's time because I know the burden of their responsibilities. But I think Chacara was grateful for the break…and I was excited to have some time to get to know her. Her voice is soft and warm. She smiles a lot. There's a twinkle in her eye and she gives the best hugs.

I also knew there was a man living in the condo with Chacara. Every time I've seen him, he is walking up and down the sidewalk with the two-year-old tucked contentedly in his arms. I've smiled to myself seeing them together and thought what a great dad he must be. The kids seem to really love him. So I was a little surprised when Chacara confessed that the man she is living with is actually her ex-husband.

They were together for twenty years. Apparently, Chacara's ex was a bit of a dog in the beginning of their relationship but when the children came, he changed, wanting to be a better man for them. There's no doubt he loves his kids, but over the years, there was a gradual shift in attention that caused Chacara to drift farther and farther into the background. Her husband was often moody. He paid more attention to his phone than to her and Chacara said he was sneaky. He would message other girls. Eventually, she just had enough. She filed for divorced…but just as the divorce was being finalized, she found out she was pregnant.

So instead of leaving the condo, she stayed. She stayed for the support. She stayed for her children and I'm sure she also stayed because of financial reasons. Her surprise baby is now two-years-old. Things between her and her ex-husband are cordial, but not fulfilling. She sleeps upstairs in the bedroom. He sleeps downstairs on the couch. Chacara said she wants to find love again. Her children, who know their parents are divorced, have voiced their desire for her to be happy and on her own. She's never had a problem finding a job when she has put her mind to it. She's been given the name of a reputable daycare for her youngest. She knows all of these things…but sometimes, it is easier to live in unhappiness than face the fear of the unknown.

She is in a rut. I know it because I, too, have been stuck like that in my life.

And it isn't as if she's weak. This is a woman that I met because she had enough experience fixing cars that she thought she could help me. This is a woman who has raised her younger siblings. Someone bright and open and friendly…but I think she knows life isn't as happy as it could be.

And the realization settled upon me that as I have been sitting in my bed over the past months, watching Netflix, feeling lonely and forgotten, right across the street was another woman likely sitting in her bed feeling lonely and forgotten, too. Our front doors are literally twenty feet away from one other! And if it wasn't for this experiment, I never would have known.

The Mask

Friend #5 – Kate

The interesting thing I've learned about meeting a person for the first time is that it usually only allows you to see them in the current moment. Whether the observer is aware of it or not, the other person's reality is colored by what is going on in their life, whether it's happy or sad or chaotic or nostalgic. If you listen closely the subconscious is drifting to whatever is at the forefront of their mind, and in a way the words passing through their lips are the reflection of their subconscious.

Typically, there is a common theme that presents itself but no one's life is comprised of just one theme. We are all made up of different parts, feelings, moods and stages of life. Our lives are a jigsaw puzzle of opposites that give our reality depth instead of reading as one flat character on a page. In the moment, we all typically wear just one mask to show the world, but sometimes, you find a rare person who will throw all the masks on at once and sit across from you wearing what might seem to be an outrageous dress-up costume, like the kind young children put together. Last Sunday, I had the pleasure of sitting across from one such enigma. Her name is Kate.

Kate went to high school with an old co-worker of mine and volunteered for this experiment. She is a brick wall of exuberance so over-powering that my first reaction was to try to move past the wall to see what makes Kate…well, Kate. And come to find out, Kate is no stranger to wearing masks.

When Kate was twelve-years-old, her father was killed by a drunk driver. He was coming back from the grocery store when a car jumped the sidewalk. One day, he was Kate's loving father and the next day he was gone. It was as shocking as if a black hole had suddenly swallowed her up. And the next morning, Kate's mother woke her and her brother and said, "Time for school." And Kate had to put on the mask that everything was normal even though her entire world had crumbled around her. As a child, she wasn't given the opportunity to grieve. She felt she had to be strong for her mother. It's the reason she has such a passion for helping children grieve now. She's become a bit of an expert on the topic, but over the last year, her mother and grandmother passed away in quick succession. "Did you take the proper time to grieve this time?" I asked and to my surprise, she said, "No". Old habits die hard.

At around the same time Kate's mother and grandmother passed away, Kate had a new boss who was hired to come into her place of employment. It didn't take long until the women clashed. Kate admitted part of the problem may have been that she hadn't taken the proper time to grieve. So now, she has to don an invisible mask of submission every week as she sits and listens to her boss lecture her about her "anger problems". The only thing Kate is really angry about is that she has to spend time listening to this woman that she fundamentally disagrees with on virtually every managerial tactic she uses. But it's a job. And she's the sole income earner. And she has kids. And that submissive mask is one a lot of us have to bear.

But there are other, happier masks, she wears, too. Kate is adventurous. When Bob Barker announced he was retiring from the Price Is Right, she gathered up a group, made it on stage and won a diamond solitaire ring, a trip to Paris and a PT Cruiser. I asked about the taxes. "Totally worth it," Kate said laughing. And once when Kate was walking down the Las Vegas Strip, she came face to face with Vanilla Ice. She grabbed him by the shoulders and shook him while screaming. "Oh my God, you're Vanilla Ice!" Of course, he promptly ran away. Kate and I agreed he probably didn't like that. Another time, she was in New York, looked over and Michael J. Fox was standing next to her. This time she calmly just said, "You're Michael J. Fox," and he gave her a look as if to say, "C'mon, lady, I'm with my kids." I guess celebrities wear masks, too.

There is a playfulness about Kate that makes me wonder if her father's death has caused her to have a delayed childhood. Or maybe she was always meant to be fun-loving. I'm not entirely sure. When Kate was at an age when most of her friends were going off to college, her best friend told her that she either needed to get serious about her life, because she was going nowhere, or they were going to have to stop being friends. To Kate's credit, she got serious and went to college, solely because she couldn't bear the thought of losing her friend. (She did choose the easiest major though.) There is such a whimsical easiness about her that you would think she'd be a pushover. That's not the case either.

Once when Kate and her family were dining in a restaurant, Kate's seven-year-old daughter asked to go to the bathroom by herself. Kate said yes because she could see the door from where she was sitting. Moments later she heard her daughter's blood curdling scream. She rushed to the restroom area not knowing what was going on and found her daughter, lying on the floor, holding her hand with blood spurting from her thumb. There was a woman coming out of the restroom just as the little girl was going in and Kate's daughter got her thumb stuck in the crevasse. The impact severed the thumb nearly off.

Kate and her husband immediately put both their daughters in the car and rushed to the nearest emergency room. It took a monumental amount of sedation to calm Kate's daughter once they reached the hospital, but once the little girl was sedated, the staff came to Kate and said they were going to have to amputate the thumb. There was just no saving it.

Kate put her foot down. "No, here's what you are going to do," she said with authority. "You are going to call a hand surgeon and after that, you are going to call a plastic surgeon. We are going to hear what they have to say and then we will make some decisions." As Kate relayed the story to me, I could see her in my mind's eye standing there like a bull, with horns lowered and nostrils flaring, an unyielding force. Two days later the hand surgeon stitched up her daughter's thumb and it has heeled nicely.

Of course, then there were medical bills. Kate reached out to the restaurant which initially appeared to be concerned but as the medical bills began to pile up, the restaurant balked. They only offered to pay one thousand dollars of the total medical costs. Kate reached out to several attorneys but apparently, because this particular restaurant was a franchise, their legal obligation was limited. Finally, Kate said, "Listen, I realize you have no legal obligation to pay these bills and I'm not looking to get rich here. I just want my daughter's medical bills paid. You can do whatever you want but just know that if these bills aren't paid, I have nothing better to do in the summer than sit outside your establishment with a sign that says my daughter severed her thumb in your restaurant." …And the medical bills were paid.

So that's Kate. She is fun-loving but headstrong. She is adventurous, laughs a lot…yet I wouldn't cross her. She is a force so strong you can literally feel it in her presence, yet she is also delightfully gentle. I spent quite a bit of time with her poking around, asking questions, feeling around for layers just beneath the surface I couldn't quite reach. I kept feeling there were doors that were locked to me as a stranger, areas of her heart and mind that maybe Kate doesn't even allow herself to explore. And that's okay. We are all a little like that. It's easier to put on a mask than to look into the dark corners of our souls, but she is real. And she is steadfast. And I look forward to more of her adventures.

The Snowbird

Friend #6 – Sherrie

My condo complex had our annual board meeting last weekend out by the pool. I know it's February but this is Phoenix, folks, so it was seventy degrees. When I arrived, there was a small gathering of homeowners milling around the donuts and coffee. Most of the people had brought lawn chairs. I plopped mine next to a dark-haired woman and said, "Mind if I sit next to you?" And that's how I met Sherrie.

In the short time before the meeting, I found out Sherrie was from Canada, she only lives here during the winter months, and she and her husband own a bunch of businesses in Canada. Once the meeting got under way, I realized Sherrie knew a lot of people in my complex. Apparently, she and her husband are well established in spending the winter months here. We call those people snowbirds in Phoenix and as the meeting droned on, I thought: I don't know any snowbirds. The purpose of this blog is to meet people who are different from me so after the meeting, I asked if she would be a willing participant in this little experiment. And she agreed.

We met at an Olive Garden restaurant not far from our condo complex. It was a Thursday night. I trudged in after a full day of work, rumpled in my jeans and t-shirt. Sherrie blew in looking crisp and refreshed in a nice black top and pants. She is from British Columbia, along the Alaskan Highway where the arctic tundra of winter is fierce this time of year. Her husband, Shane, who was up there checking on their businesses, told her it was negative twenty-five degrees that morning. That, in itself, was enough to make me understand why Sherrie might enjoy it down in Phoenix during the winter. But it's not just the cold that gets to Sherrie. Those from the Pacific Northwest know the sun rarely comes out between the months of September and May, and Sherrie, like many people, suffers from depression when she doesn't get enough sunshine.

Her husband, on the other hand, travels back and forth during the winter. Sherrie says she doubts he will ever retire. Shane's father started the family truck company with just one dump truck many years ago. By the time Sherrie's husband was sixteen, he had his own truck. He and his siblings have now grown the business into a thriving company with almost forty trucks…but it wasn't easy. With a family business, it is hard to know where the family ends and the business begins, and when Sherrie came into the family, twenty-nine years ago, she quickly realized the decisions she and her husband made as a family were sometimes overshadowed by the will of other family members. Sherrie's mother-in-law, in a particular, had a rough time accepting that her son had a family of his own.

In a way, it was a rather traditional life where Sherrie raised their three children and Shane went off to work, but the life of a business owner doesn't necessarily stop at a certain hour of the day. Often, Shane would be gone for long periods of time, leaving Sherrie to play both mother and father to their children. Any mother will tell you raising children is strenuous work, and during those times when Shane was gone, Sherrie would also have to deal with business matters at home. It was tough. And it was even more difficult when

Canada's economy hit the skids and the business started to flounder. They kept their employees on as long as they could, finding them odd jobs to do around the office but eventually, there was no getting around it. Financially, they had to let some people go. These were hard workers that were loyal to the company. Sherrie and Shane agonized over the decision and finally agreed to keep only those workers who had families to support, although it was a difficult decision all the way around.

But the economy came back around and business started to pick up again. Sherrie's children grew up and now have children of their own. Of course, she's still a doting mother…and grandmother. During our dinner, her youngest daughter called and I could hear the warmth in Sherrie's voice as they briefly spoke. When she hung up, Sherrie told me her daughter struggled with a weight problem for most of her life but over the last two years, her daughter has lost a ton of weight and transformed her body. Sherrie showed me pictures and proudly told me how her daughter now wants to find ways to motivate others to do the same. This is the daughter that now runs their gym. I could tell how proud Sherrie is of her.

Sherrie and Shane now have other business ventures, too. In addition to the gym, they also own a carwash and another business involving grills (I think). When the kids all left home, Sherrie started an antique boutique shop with a friend of hers that she helped run until her mother grew ill. Nowadays, Sherrie's life isn't ruled by timeframes. She goes and comes as she pleases. They own a few properties down here in the U.S. and a motor home that allows them to travel around.

And as Sherrie was telling me all of this, it occurred to me that I'm sitting across from her at an Olive Garden, our condo complex is far from flashy, and Sherrie isn't really that much older than I am. She's very modest yet engaging. She's also the first person to tell you that she knows she's fortunate. I was a little in awe because I don't know anyone else with that type of freedom! I took a moment to take stock of my emotions and as I was faltering, she said, "Well, that's it," as if to apologize to me. As if her life wasn't very interesting. I was little dumbfounded in my envy. What struck me the most wasn't the fact that she has the financial security to do what she pleases or the freedom of her time. What struck me the most was something she said very early on in our conversation...

Her husband had called her that morning and said, "You know, I miss you. I can't wait to see you." Sherrie told me that even after twenty-nine years of marriage they still love being in each other's company. It is eminently apparent that Sherrie has the type of deep, loving relationships that I've failed miserably at attaining. It would mean so much to me if anyone enjoyed my company enough to miss me. And as I hugged Sherrie goodbye, I left with a sense of hope...because if there is one person in this world who is truly loved then maybe, just maybe, there is hope for me yet.

The Healer

Friend #7 – Adrian

I did it. I did the thing I said I was not going to do.

I don't know if it was because Valentine's Day was coming up. Maybe I just ran into one too many happy couples…but the old, lonely hole opened up in my heart reminding me I'm a single. And then I got the itch to want to shop the dating sites. I tried to resist. For hours, I begged the television to entertain me but the pull was just too great. I'd done a very good job at deleting all of my information on the dating sites so I didn't have access. It took some work to put up a new profile with no photo, no description, just meant to look, but moments into the process I realized…I wasn't missing much. I was just about to log out when I noticed someone had sent me a message.

It was harmless enough, just a question about the screen name I chose. I looked at his profile. It said he was open to making new friends so I figured…why not? Here's a guy willing to take a chance not even knowing what I look like. And that's how I met Adrian.

We chose to meet at a Mexican restaurant in Mesa. Adrian said he grew up just across the canal, but that was a different time when Mesa was considered rural. My first impression was that he was meek and mild mannered with a soft voice, not a bad looking guy, but just underneath the surface I could feel a controlled anger, seeping around the edges like a noxious gas. He said his brother had just sent him a text that ticked him off so it is entirely possible that I caught him in a bad moment in time. But even if it was just the moment, Adrian still has a lot to be angry about.

He has primary custody of his children, ages thirteen, eleven and nine because their mother's boyfriend physically and emotionally abused them. His youngest is special needs so every day at 3 pm Adrian has to be there to meet the bus, which means he can really only work five hours a day. It's hard to get ahead on a schedule like that. And to make matters worse, his ex-wife refuses to pay child support…yet still manages to drive a Mercedes.

And he's a talented guy. For a lot of his life, he's been a contractor. He showed me photos of his work. I could see in the photos his precision and creativity. He has also designed swimwear and from those photos, I couldn't tell the difference between his work and Victoria's Secret. Without saying it, I sensed a sensitive, creative soul, but his most incredible talent may be something called KST.

"KST is a healing protocol used to locate and correct/release areas of blockage, distortion, subluxation, interference, stagnation and other stresses in the body and body/mind that are often missed by most healthcare professionals," according to the website, www.korenspecifictechnique.com. As I sat across from Adrian at dinner, he began examining me in what almost seemed like a trance. He noted three places on my body that were out of whack including my collar bone, my hip bone and the bones in my right foot. I hadn't told him I'm a runner that often leads with my right foot and he never moved from his side of the table to look at my hip or my feet. He also showed me testimonials of people he has helped. As strange as it sounds, I believed him. I believe he does have a gift.

Before Adrian and his ex-wife had children, they lived in New Mexico. He found work in a restaurant, hoping to one day become a chef. He started as a host, was quickly promoted to a waiter and then within two months, was running the entire operation. The customers loved him! They were important people in the community who came in specifically to request his service. It was the happiest time in Adrian's life. One day, the owner came to him and offered him a house and a forty thousand dollar a year salary to try to persuade Adrian to stay instead of going to culinary school, but one of the chefs took Adrian aside. His coworker told him the owner planned to turn him into a slave to the restaurant, a position Adrian would never be able to leave, no matter how resentful he eventually became. So Adrian turned the offer down. He said he now regrets that decision.

Adrian also has some interesting ideas about life, in general. He believes people should not be dependent on other sources for their nourishment, in case the worst happens. He has a strong belief in Bitcoin as the currency of the future and he is curious about other subversive rumors that seem to forecast a bleak future. He is also vehemently repulsed by the entitled. Adrian's grandmother came to this country from Mexico after the Mexican Revolution. All of the men in her family had been killed and she spent her life in labor camps migrating from Arizona to California to pick crops. She worked hard and instilled that work ethic in her family. "No one is owed anything" Adrian said …but on that point…I think he is wrong.

We are all owed respect. And we all deserve to be seen, something I don't think Adrian has personally experienced very often. I think his natural meekness has caused him to blend into the crowd. I think the jeers and the put-downs and the under-the-breath slurs people have cast upon him have damaged his sensitive soul to the point that he puts on a coat of anger in order to reject people before they reject him. That way it doesn't hurt so much. I think he's angry because deep down he knows he is worthy and talented, but he doesn't know how to make other people see it. I think his entire being is screaming out to be recognized for the talented individual he is. And yes, he does have some unusual beliefs but the greatest minds in history did too.

I hugged him goodbye in the dark parking lot of that Mexican restaurant in Mesa, knowing it wasn't a love connection, knowing he probably already felt rejected by me, but I also really wanted to help him. I wanted him to know that someone really listened and appreciated him for the man he is. His real passion is healing people who are in pain and I think if there were more people who could see his abilities, the healer, in essence, would be healed. I believe there is a lot of love in this world. Adrian just hasn't had enough of his share of it.

The Witch

Friend #8 – Sandy

When I first set out on this meeting-new-people adventure, one of my friends came to me and said, "I want you to sit down with Sandy but she is about to go undergo surgery for breast cancer. Can you wait a couple of months?"

Of course, I could wait.

I wanted to know what it was like to be hit with the heavy weight of a cancer diagnosis. I had heard that Sandy was doing much better now so when I sat down with her in a Starbucks on a chilly Sunday morning, my first question was ripped right out of an old Tim McGraw song: "How does it hit you when you get that kind of news?"

I was prepared for earth shattering trauma but Sandy just shrugged and said, "I'm seventy. Things like that are to be expected." In a shockingly honest display of her own mortality, Sandy went on to explain that she realizes she is probably closer to the end of her life than the beginning. And while the burning sensation in her arms is annoying and the hair loss still forces her to wear a wig, she is happy to be feeling more like herself. She also understands that a cancer diagnosis for some people can be more overwhelming but, in her heart, she always believed it was going to be alright. Even in the beginning.

I asked her how she could have so much faith and she explained to me it was because she is a witch.

Wait…what?!?

It took me a beat or two to recover from that one.

When Sandy was twenty years old, a glowing entity came to her and said, "We mean you no harm". Since then, strange things happen around Sandy. Lights come on and off without anyone touching the switch. Washing machines come on for no reason. Knives pull out of their holders and lay down on the counter…and that's just a few of the strange things that happen. She has a sense of being surrounded by spirits but because it's been going on for so long, it has become her normal.

Years ago, Sandy was married to a man who was a house painter. There was one particular house where the job began small and then got bigger…and bigger. Sandy and her husband became good friends with the couple who owned the house. The two couples even had dinner together. But unbeknownst to Sandy, her husband was having an affair with the woman who owned that house and eventually Sandy's husband left her to be with the other woman. Sandy was devastated! So, in order to heal her broken heart, she found herself drifting towards alternative treatments, sources that involved energy like reiki, crystals and herbs. She was accustomed to feeling outside energy since spirits had surrounded her for most of her life. And in her journey to heal herself, Sandy met a number of women who were also interested in energy healing methods. They didn't come all at once. They came one at a time but after a while, Sandy began to notice that many of the women she consorted with, who believed as she believed, were witches.

For her, witchcraft is less about a religion and more about a lifestyle. She isn't quiet about her beliefs, although many of her friends are. She doesn't belong to a coven...yet she labels herself as a witch. And the women who surround her have become her best support. As a seventy-year-old woman facing cancer without a spouse, Sandy needed help over the last few months. She's had people who have cooked for her, sat with her during her chemo treatments. She even had one friend come over to pick up the dog poop in her backyard. These women, fifteen or so in number, have created a supportive community structure, leaving Sandy no opportunities other than just to get better. She credits these women's healing energy for having paved her way away from cancer.

"It's a funny thing," she said. "Be careful for what you wish for."

Apparently, in the years leading up to her cancer diagnosis, Sandy said she often wished she could lose twenty-five pounds and be able to afford a boob job. Now that cancer is in the rearview mirror, she realizes she has lost twenty-five pounds because of her lack of appetite and along with her mastectomy, came a free boob job. Sandy laughed at the irony in a way that made me love her and as I sat with her, I found myself being absorbed by her energy. There was calm. There was peace. But mostly, there was love in this woman who lives her life outside of the customary boundaries.

The Tough Cookie
Friend #9 – Amanda

Strength comes in many different forms.

Amanda was a starry-eyed ASU freshman when a friend of hers asked her to go on a church trip to San Diego. Even though Amanda had never been particularly religious, a trip to San Diego sounded pretty good to her. It was on that trip that she met the man she would eventually marry. He was Russian, here in Arizona on a work visa. He was fourteen-years her elder and he was deliciously exotic.

Unfortunately, this isn't a love story.

Amanda's Russian admitted he was really only interested in the church so he could meet girls. Amanda is a brassy, no-nonsense New Yorker so I doubt she was ever naïve…but at the time, she was young and she didn't really recognize the power the age difference would hold over her. She dated her Russian on and off for four years and then when she was twenty-one and nearing her college graduation, she found out she was pregnant.

She had wanted to go to grad school but her Russian wanted to get married. There was no pressure from Amanda's family but there is a persistent societal pressure for women to get married after college. It seemed to be the next step. Being pregnant, it was only natural that Amanda would want to check that box off her list. She thought it was for her benefit…and for the baby's. So even though she had a degree in social work, Amanda married her Russian, had a son and was relegated to a housewife…and slowly Amanda's life drifted into what was expected…but not what made her happy.

Amanda now wonders if it was really love or the desire to try to do the right thing that kept her moving deeper and deeper into the Russian's clutches. He was selfish and unkind. Amanda said she was in the delivery room having their second child when she realized she wanted to divorce her husband. Three months later she was sitting across from a divorce attorney.

Amanda believes a lot of women would have lived with the unhappiness. She had two small children and no income. All of her family was back east so there was no one to help her. There was no one to give her emotional or financial support when she needed it. She didn't say it because she's such a tough cookie but she must have been scared. She probably had to dig down deep inside of her herself to find the strength to leave, not knowing what would happen next. I respect that kind of moxie. I respect it because I know exactly what it takes…because I, too, have had to find that strength.

Amanda found a job with the State and over the past two years, she has done her best to put herself in a better place. A lot of the time she has been exhausted from work, from her children, from just trying to keep her head above water as a single mom. But in September, she began to feel a little more stable. She began to be open to meeting someone new. She lost twenty pounds. She started online dating and most people would think that's where the story ends.

And then Amanda said this:
"How do you make yourself vulnerable when you've already been hurt so badly?"

Of all the things she's been through, vulnerability is the thing she struggles with the most. Being tough...or at least making people think you are tough is easy...but how do you purposely make yourself vulnerable knowing you are giving a stranger the power to hurt you?

I don't really know the answer but if determination and gumption have anything to do with it, Amanda will find a way. She's already happier. And she's hopeful that somewhere out there is a person who will love her for the woman she is. And where there is hope, there is always possibility.

The Accidental Friends

Friends #10 & #11 – Heather & Dr. Evil

Dear Friends,

I need to catch you up on all that has happened over the last month since my last posting. You may have thought I have given up on the idea of making 52 new friends this year. That could not be farther from the truth. But here's what I have learned: As I get deeper and deeper into this process, I find people are reluctant to sit down with me. I've got a backlog six or seven deep of women who liked the idea enough to agree to sit down with me, but, for one reason or another, have not made the time to do it.

Part of me has been in mourning over it because how sad is our society that people are so overtaxed that they don't even have time to schedule in one hour to talk about themselves and meet a new friend. Or maybe the idea of having someone write about them is too daunting? Or maybe they just don't want to be my friend and don't know how to tell me? Or maybe something else is holding them back? I don't know. These are all guesses. But it makes me feel bad.

I feel like I'm disappointing all of you who have read this blog and given me encouragement. I feel like I've disappointed myself on not achieving a goal. And then it hit me… Without being formal, I have continued to make friends. So you are now entering a series of blogs where I will talk about people that I didn't realize I was getting to know.

We are going to start with my accidental friends…

About a month ago, one of my Facebook friends messaged me and asked me to lunch. I said yes…because I'm always about the yes, but as the designated time drew near, I started to realize that I couldn't remember how Heather and I had met. We've been Facebook friends for at least seven years. We've shot messages back and forth over the social network. I know we are both part of the sorority alumnae association…and that's just about it.

And then I got nervous…because I didn't know what she was going to want from me.

We had apparently met when our sorority was re-colonizing at ASU. In order for that to happen, they needed alumnae help and I had volunteered. I remember it because it was the one time I actually wore my wedding ring. I'm the child of farm people who physically work hard enough that wearing a wedding ring may mean that a finger gets caught in a piece of machinery or lost in a pile of ick. So wearing a wedding ring was never important when I was married except in situations, like that night, when I was going to run into a lot of people I didn't know who might question why I wasn't wearing a ring.

That's it. That's all I remember.

At lunch, Heather and I talked a lot about my work and my dating life. I'm a nervous chatterer. I'm pretty sure I talked too much and listened too little. But Heather was patient. She recently stepped down as an alumnae chapter advisor for our sorority after having served a lot of years. I think she may have a hole in her life that she's struggling to fill. She heard I was looking to make more friends and well, that's how I got to know Heather a lot better than I did. And as it turns out, she's pretty darn cool.

But soon boredom took over in my spare time and I, again, began peeping into the online dating scene through the profile I created with nothing on it. I had just about come to the conclusion that I wasn't missing anything when I suddenly got a message. It only said, "Hi", but the sender happened to be extremely good looking. If he'd been ugly, I probably wouldn't have responded. Instead, I messaged back.

"What are you doing messaging a girl with no photo? I could be a five-hundred-pound wart hog. You don't know! You are a good-looking dude. I'm sure you will have plenty of gorgeous women messaging you if they haven't already."

But that seemed to intrigue him even more.

So again, I pushed back. "Listen, I'm not really looking to date right now. I'm broken. I'm sure you will find someone who is a better fit."

Not even that deterred him.

And to his credit, he was a good enough salesman that he talked me into a date. I had to do a mad dash to get to the restaurant on time because at work they announced, with only a day's notice, that we were having a pot luck lunch the next day. I'd whipped together a couple of pies that were cooling on my stove as I walked up to the quaint little restaurant he'd picked out. It was a lovely little house someone had converted and we sat in what was essentially the front yard, under a large shade tree strung with twinkle lights. He picked out some wine. We had deep, intellectual conversation. He told me all about his smart twenty-four-year-old daughter that he raised on his own. She wants to go to law school, go into politics and change the world…and he couldn't be prouder.

For one brief moment, as he talked about his cat, I couldn't help but look at his bald head, his shiny eyes and think of Dr. Evil from the Austin Power's movies. Thus, he will always be known to me as Dr. Evil. We took a walk after dinner. He kissed me lightly before we parted ways.

And the next morning, I woke up with explosive diarrhea.

I think it may have been the wine. But being unsure of the origination of such a disaster, I determined I could not take those two pies I made into work. They were now sick pies, possibly contaminated with germilogical foreign bodies.

Dr. Evil never called me again.

And I spent the next week gorging myself on those two pies I didn't have the heart to throw away.

Oh well. I wasn't supposed to be dating anyway.

The Old Soul
Friend #12 – Sarah

There are old souls that inhabit the earth, beings of youth who exhibit such natural wisdom that one starts to wonder if they really even fit in this generation of selfies and YouTube makeup tutorials.

I met Sarah by working with a local non-profit. She is the type of unyielding dependable that you never have to worry about anything being left undone. She's a little bit of 'Little House on the Prairie' with her long, blond hair and her natural heart-shaped face. Her voice is soft. Her eyes are warm. She's the type of person you instantly feel you have known for years.

You'd think she was from the Midwest from that description but Sarah actually grew up near Buffalo, New York, surrounded by farms for as far as the eye could see. She loved to ride horses. In fact, for a while, she considered becoming a horse trainer but she never had a horse of her own. She was raised by a single mom and horses are expensive. So Sarah learned her skills by riding and taking care of other people's horses. It didn't mean she loved it any less.

She moved out to California for college with big dreams of working with professional athletes but an internship in the community relations department of a professional sports team changed all that. What Sarah really loved was connecting with people, forming meaningful relationships. She realized that the important things in life were not the materialistic ones. It was the people in her life. It was the people she could help. So Sarah changed her focus and after college began working in the non-profit world.

With her long blond hair, you would think Sarah would be the quintessential beach beauty, perfectly fit for Orange County but Sarah has a simple, rhythmic beat to her life that doesn't match the crowded alcoves of Southern California. In fact, she always felt a bit out of place. She was looking to escape when a friend of hers took her to a party where she met her friend's boss…and fell madly in love.

Kevin builds medical technological devices that help us live. He's a smart guy with a solid income and, like Sarah, simple in his own way. There were numerous times when their paths should have crossed in ways reminiscent of "How I Met Your Mother". Once, Sarah stayed with some friends in a room that had been vacated by the roommate for the weekend. Turns out, it was Kevin's room. He was the roommate. They both moved to Arizona for a while but their entire four-year relationship has been plagued with distance. It never deterred them or weakened their commitment to one another.

So when Kevin moved back to California in January for a job, it never occurred to him to leave Sarah behind. But Sarah wasn't thrilled about the idea of living in California again. To her, California represented all of the materialistic things that she is not...even though Kevin settled in Northern California, which is very different than the southernmost part of the state.

Kevin found a cute little house nestled onto twelve hundred acres for them to live in with plenty of room for Sarah and her Siberian Husky, Molson, to explore. Still, Sarah struggled to let go of her feminist side, the one that demanded her independence. Sarah's mother had always been her role model of making it on her own, yet the tender whisperings of husband and family were whispering in her ear, pulling her back towards the west coast. And then Kevin uttered the words to the vision that would finally make Sarah's decision complete: There was enough land and resources for Sarah to finally have a horse of her own. For Sarah, it would be the completion of a dream.

As Sarah told me the story, I realized this was Sarah's goodbye to me…but it is the beginning of a beautiful new chapter of her life. She will again live amongst farmland. She will be able to cultivate the deep, personal relationships she loves to have. She has found a job at another non-profit that she believes will be even more fulfilling than the one she left behind. And maybe…just maybe…there will be a ring. The discussion, at least, has been there.

At the end of this week, Sarah will move and the Arizona chapter in her life will close. And for me, for once, I'm just happy to be a part of a happy ending.

The Millennials
Friends #13 & #14

This past Sunday, I attended an inspiring talk at ASU about the Power of Passion. It's an interesting topic and as I listened to each speaker, I realized living life is my passion. You never know what it's going to bring! In the past, I have felt sorry for the generations that come behind me. So many people talk about how the millennials and generation z are failing. I've read articles about how technology has not prepared these generations for hard work...or life, in general. It's as if these generations lack passion. And then, when I least expect it, my job takes me a direction that allows me to meet people in their twenties who have learned to harness their passion and succeed.

Unfortunately, both of these people I've had the privilege to get to know live in the public eye, so to keep them anonymous I am going to call them 'Ann' and 'Andy'.

'Ann' is a twenty-eight-year-old real estate agent. She was on her way to get her master's degree when she took a summer job working for a real estate company and just fell in love with it. Suddenly her focus changed and she couldn't see herself doing anything outside of real estate. One of 'Ann's' other passions is hiking. Late last year, 'Ann' heard about a special interest group that was looking to use money marked for sustaining the preserve she loved to build a tourist attraction right in the middle of protected land. Not only would the attraction be an eye soar for nature lovers but it would also, in essence, bankrupt the fund that has been keeping the land preserved. 'Ann' was outraged! So she decided to do something. She began working with a group lobbying to keep the attraction from coming to fruition and that's when 'Ann' began to notice, she was, by far, the youngest person in the room.

She began to notice that people her own age weren't paying attention. They would wave her off when she asked them to sign a petition. They never wanted to listen when she tried to instill the importance of her fight. It bothered her so much that 'Ann' decided she wanted to do something about it…so she decided to make herself an example. She decided to run for political office. More important than getting elected is her desire to save the preserve she loves and to encourage other people her age to live their most passionate lives by changing the world around them.

I'd like to call 'Ann' a revolutionary but just before I met her, I was fortunate enough to have a drink with another millennial setting the world on fire.

'Andy' readily admits he always wanted to be on a platform. But how do you get that job? After graduating from college, he worked a bunch of low-paying odd jobs, none of which was even close to the spotlight. In fact, he was working in a call center when someone asked him if he'd heard about the contest a local radio station was running to compete for the chance to become an on-air personality. 'Andy' had no idea what they were talking about, but he went home and looked it up.

To qualify, a contestant first had to submit a video. So 'Andy' uploaded his video to the station two days before the deadline and got a call to come in and audition. He just knew this was his big break, but when he got to the studio, he realized he was among a large group of contestants. The afternoon DJ, was checking in each contestant as they arrived. Star struck, 'Andy' said, "Oooh...I love your hair!" which was pink.

The woman scowled as if 'Andy' had just insulted her. "What do you mean by that?"

"Oooh...uh...just that I like your hair," he said wilting under the woman's glare. She checked him in and 'Andy' went to the back of the room. He put his back to the wall and slid down to the floor, certain he had just blown his shot. When they called him up to try out, he auditioned and then he went home.

Three weeks after the audition, the station's programming director called 'Andy' asking him if he wanted to sit in on the morning show for a week trial. There was just one problem: 'Andy' had a full time job and no vacation time.

He thought about calling in sick but he knew someone would hear him on the radio and rat him out. So he came clean, told his employer what was going on and they agreed to let him temporarily work the night shift. Morning radio begins EARLY so 'Andy' needed to be in the studio by 5 AM. He would work his shift at the radio station, be at his call center job by 2 PM, leave work at 10 PM only to go home and try to get a little sleep.

By midweek, the station decided they wanted him on the air permanently...but there was a catch. They could only hire him as part time. For a while, 'Andy' kept up the impossible schedule of having two jobs until he just couldn't function any longer. After three months, he put in his resignation at the call center and lived on a part-time wage. As 'Andy's' star began to rise, he was actually living in poverty. He couldn't afford to go anywhere so he spent most of his free time alone and depressed. He used up his entire savings during his first year in radio and just when he felt like it was about to break him, the station decided to hire him full time.

Today, you can hear 'Andy' on the radio every morning. He has become a highly popular figure and has been an inspiration to a number of young people. And as he grows his following, the sky really is the limit but it couldn't have happened without hard work and a passion to succeed.

Neither 'Ann' nor 'Andy' really wanted me to tell their stories. This wasn't my typical 'friend' setup. But each of these individuals was so inspiring to me, that I simply could not just idly let these stories sit. I think it is important for millennials and generation z to realize the world is changing, leaders are emerging and because of them, the world will one day be a better place than the way my generation left it.

The Excommunicated

Friend #15 – Ben

Ben grew up in a Mormon family. He and his twin sister were the middle children out of six. Ben did all the things that good Mormon boys do. When he was of age, he went on his mission. He came back and got married. He and his wife had three children who were perfectly planned exactly two years apart from one another. Ben followed the scriptures. He studied at night to get his bachelor's degree online…and then his masters. He was well liked among his fellow Mormons. He was well liked by everyone. So when Ben was asked to be a leader in his church, he graciously took the position. It was a great honor.

But one day, Ben consciously had a thought that should never have entered his religiously conditioned brain. As devote as he and his family were to prayer and the scriptures, he could not find the answer to his prayers anywhere in his everyday life.

Ben didn't voice this thought…but it was there, gnawing away at his faith. He got to the point where in prayer meetings he would lean back, cross his arms and look around the room at all of the bowed heads. He just didn't feel like he thought he should inside.

One day, as he was sitting in church, he was looking around the room when he felt something shift. It was like he was being lifted up over the crowd and was looking down at the people of the church below. He felt as if he knew something they did not, and from that day forward, his internal belief system changed to embrace science over faith.

Still, he kept up appearances. He smiled in family photos. But there was so much about his life that brought him unhappiness. He owned a business that failed. The relationship he had with his wife was mostly for appearances. He walked through life feeling empty. And then one day, he had an affair. It was short-lived but still a rebellion. He tried to do the right thing. He came clean but his wife immediately packed up her belongings, took their children and left to stay with her sister. A week later, Ben received the divorce papers.

The church came to Ben and told him that he needed to make reparations for his actions. They still loved him and accepted him as their brother but there had to be consequences. They gave Ben a number of different options that he could pursue…or they told him he could be excommunicated.

Ben chose to be excommunicated. That means he won't be able to go into the Mormon Temple when his children marry. It means he separated himself from everything he has ever known.

Ben now lives with the shadow of the Temple hovering over him and little by little, he is finding himself. In a lot of ways, he is still naïve to the ways of the world. Things like drinking a cup of coffee still throw him for a loop, like he's doing something wrong. But other things, he gladly gave up. One of those things was the traditional Mormon undergarments that he wore for more than twenty years. He always found them to be restricting and uncomfortable. Now, on weekends, when his children are away with their mother, he confessed he sometimes just sits around naked because it makes him feel free…and because, well, now he can.

The Wedding Date

Friends #16 & #17 – Brian & Lou

My friend, Katie, was getting married. At the end of March, she sent me at text that read: "What is the name of your plus one? We are doing the place cards and need to know."

I read the text like a deer in headlights. Six months ago, when I RSVP'd, I had a debate on whether or not to mark the plus one box. I had decided to air on the side of optimism and I marked the box. Six months later, and still single, I had no idea who I was going to bring.

"Well…" I stammered over text. "I thought I still had some time."

"Well…" Katie texted back. "We are less than a month out now. Soooo…we probably need to know…"

I looked up at the sky and wiped both my palms all the way down my face….as if that was going to make me feel any better. "I have an idea," I texted back. "You are the bride so tell me if this is going to ruin your wedding…but what if we put on the place card 'Mystery Date'? And then I'm not locked into anyone specific."

Katie texted back, "I love it!" And the hunt was on.

At first, I looked for guy friends who might be available. That came to screeching halt pretty quickly. So since I was out of options, I decided to throw up a dating profile with my specific request of needing a wedding date, that way I could quickly weed out anyone who wouldn't want to go. I got a slew of messages but these were my top two:

Brian spent most of his life in St. Louis. He has a grown daughter, a couple of grandchildren and six months ago, decided to re-start his life here in Phoenix where it is warm all year long. He thought it would be easier to find an IT job out here than it was. He had to eat through a lot of his savings to make the transition. But when I met him, he'd just started a new job that he seemed to really like. He was excited to be in Phoenix where he could ride his Harley more often and meet other Harley enthusiasts. He was also just as handsome in person as he was in his photos online.

Lou was an admitted wanderer. After a record-setting income year for him in tech sales, Lou decided to quit his job and travel around the world. He literally took a year to travel wherever his heart took him and now he's back in the United States to restart his career…because, you know, we all need money to survive. He's intelligent, a deep-thinker with a big heart and huge, contagious smile. He married once when he was in the Navy, which was more a marriage of convenience than for love. He never had children but is content to take things as they come.

They were both lovely. I ended up choosing Lou because we seemed to have more in common but the truth was that neither were really a love match. I wanted it to be there but it was just a chemistry thing. It kind of pissed me off.

There's the old breakup line that everyone knows: It isn't you, it's me. But I really think it IS me. I've always been the biggest advocate that no matter how much someone hurts you, you should keep your heart open because you never know when someone else who is wonderful will step in and fill your heart with all the love and kindness you've always wanted. That advice has served others well. It's done crap for me.

I know I've consciously kept the door to my heart open but my heart has also been through a lot of damage.

There was the one who spent all my money and left me penniless.

There was the one who was so selfish and complacent that it cost me my fertility.

There was the one that cared more about being drunk and high than any little problem I had.

And there was the one that in a fit of supreme emotional abuse and manipulation, threw me out of that house in the middle of the night with no place to go.

I want to be happy so I choose to no longer dwell in those hurtful memories. Over the past two and a half years, I've been more single than I've ever been in my entire adult life. I have invited a few into my heart only to be brutally rejected. Maybe the door to my heart is now covered with an impenetrable scar tissue that is keeping everyone out, not allowing me to feel...well...anything.

Maybe every girl doesn't get her Prince Charming. That doesn't mean I'm going to live my life with anything less than being full. It will come when it comes. Or it won't. And either way I will move forward with a happiness of my own making.

The Cool Chick

Friend #18 – Shawn

People are fascinating to me. Every time I sit down with someone new, I never know what to expect and the conversation always seems to take on a life of its own.

I met Shawn through a friend of mine who happens to be her hairstylist. The three of us had hung out once before but this is the first time she and I had met one-on-one. Some people you greet with a handshake because you can feel the emotional distance. That's normal. Occasionally, you run into someone you immediately feel enough closeness with that a hug seems more appropriate. And every now and then, you will run into someone you feel like you can immediately share your innermost secrets with. A sort of love at first sight, I guess.

That's how Shawn was for me. Maybe with her infectious smile and warm personality, she's like that for everyone. It was how she met her husband.

Immediately, we fell into a conversation of all the things we, as women, do to tear each other down.

We started with the mother/daughter relationship, which hasn't been my strong suit. Shawn and I are both children of

Southern mothers, who raised us to be Southern debutantes in rural areas where there were no cotillions or fancy dresses or declarations of class. There was only suffocating control reminding me of a line in a Miranda Lambert song: "It doesn't matter how you feel, it only matters how you look."

When Shawn's mother became elderly, all the issues and responsibilities surrounding the elderly came falling down on Shawn's shoulders. She had always considered her mother to be a needy woman but when her mother's health started to fail, Shawn had a difficult time keeping up with all of her mother's demands. She felt like it was her duty to help but the relationship with her mother left her feeling drained and overwhelmed, like she was never good enough. Shawn began to resent her mother and became so emotional about it that she finally sought the advice of a therapist.

Only then did she realize her feelings were valid. The mother/daughter relationship always seems complicated but some people have an easier time navigating through it than others. A mother seems to have the ability to either build up or tear down a daughter with a flick of a word on the tongue. Unfortunately, not all mothers use that power for the good of the daughter. There are mothers who tear into the daughter because of their own insecurities, not realizing the damage they leave in their wake. Shawn had a mother like this. So do I. Yet it is the foundation of what a woman's self-worth is based on.

I once attended a seminar where we talked about the things that make women most vulnerable. Not being able to balance and be great at everything was at the top of the list. Which is ridiculous. Because who is great at everything? Shawn never had the biological need to have children. It just wasn't a role she wanted to take on, but being childless myself, I can relate to how a group of women can make you feel inferior because you are childless. In our society, being childless means you have failed at being a woman and inevitably, other women have the need to reach out and console you for your shortcomings. "You still have time…" is a phrase I've heard a lot.

In Shawn's case, she is childless by choice. It doesn't make her less of a woman. It actually makes her a more self-aware person to step out of society's box of what a woman should be and focus on those things that make her uniquely her. Instead of having children of her own, Shawn has worked on having a healthy marriage and has helped raise her stepchildren, both admirable aspects of life that she might not have been able to do so fluidly if she had children of her own.

And since we were on the topic of insecurities, Shawn whispered, "I'm not like you. I know I would never feel confident in the workplace." First of all, that made me laugh because the implication was that I have my life in order, but it also opened up another area where Shawn has felt the judgment of other women. For most of her married life, Shawn has been a housewife. She knows all too well the things women whisper under their breath about her. It's probably the things you are thinking right now…

I won't print them here because I know how hurtful those sharp little words are to Shawn.

And yet, as she was sitting in front of me, all I could see was an intelligent, seemingly happy woman who made me smile. She made me think a little deeper about all the things we, as women, subconsciously do to each other to make us feel inadequate. We perpetuate that myth that a woman must be good at everything when shouldn't our purpose in this world be to nurture and be happy? Shawn taught me a little about all of that. I guess, every now and then, a person comes along who changes the way you look at the world and because of her, the paradigm of my world shifted…and I can't wait to see where the rest of the friendship takes us.

The Scientist

Friend #19 – Charley

Charley has always been good at figuring things out.

He was once traveling to Roswell, New Mexico. His flight landed after the sun had set. He rented a car and while driving down the long, narrow road into Roswell, he saw a mysterious glow in the sky that seemed to be following him. Anyone that knows anything about Roswell, New Mexico might think that Charley was experiencing a U.F.O. But Charley doesn't believe in such things. He kept studying the eerie orb from his vantage point behind the steering wheel, wondering what exactly it could be. When he finally reached the town, itself, he realized the glow was actually the city's lights being reflected off the low-hanging mist. The slight curvature of road he was traveling gave the impression that the lights were following him. I asked him if he believed that this may have been the cause of a lot of U.F.O. sightings in the Roswell area. And he said, 'yes'.

While in Roswell, he happened to meet the son of the neighbor of the farmer who originally found an object that fell from the sky. The man told Charley no one thought much of it until the newspapers got involved. Charley believes this is where the propaganda and conspiracies about U.F.O.'s started. Instead of factual accuracy, there were a few who profited off of the idea of aliens landing on earth based on a singular event which could have been cause by something very simple.

Charley has figured other things out, as well. He once had a woman tell him that while she was in Canada, she and a friend had a spiritual experience close to a frozen lake. They were walking towards the lake when a force that she could only describe as sound waves, physically pushed them out onto it. Charley sighed, knowing there had to be an explanation. He began asking questions about what the woman saw and heard in the moments before this spiritual experience, and the woman told him she did hear a loud rumbling immediately before the event. It was Charley who deduced that on the other side of the mountain behind her, there must have been an avalanche just out of eyesight. The force of the tumbling snow caused the powerful sound waves that pushed her out onto the lake. And the mystery was solved.

Charley enjoys these real-life brain teasers. He likes the way the laws of nature have absolute certainty. And yet, there is one mystery in his life that constantly challenges his ordered existence. His thirteen-year-old son has Asperger's Disease.

Charley can study the disease. He can study its symptoms. He can study medications and treatments. But he cannot control the devastating irregularities of the actions of his son. I asked him if he had wanted more children but he said he and his wife could barely keep up with the child they had. He described his young son like three children all in one.

And so, for all the order and tidiness in Charley's life, there is this one little thing that will never make sense in an otherwise orderly universe, a peculiar irregularity that can never be solved.

The Adventurer
Friend #20 – Christine

It was a beautiful evening in downtown Mesa. Spring was just starting to melt into the heat of the summer. I'd been invited to the Mesa Arts Center for their Season Preview, a rather exclusive event. When I entered the theater, I had to take a moment to adjust my perception. A group of round tables covered in white tablecloths were gathered onto the stage. A flamingo dancer was performing to the sound of a solitary guitar. I was in awe as I made my way up onto the stage, as if I were entering into the performance, itself.

I was standing in line for the buffet when someone from the Mesa Arts Center introduced Christine to me. We both work in the same industry and had come to the event alone. I'm sure it seemed like an easy pairing…and it was.

While we waited in the lengthy line, Christine told me she had only been in Phoenix for the past two and a half months. She was working in San Diego when the opportunity came up for her to transfer to Phoenix, which is a bigger market. She said she already loved it here, that she was still feeling like she was on vacation. And her smile told it all. Christine has a very easy way about her that draws you in, a calming presence that reminds you of the girl next door. She's quick witted, a sharp judge of character…and she was an easy friend in a room where I didn't know anyone else.

Over dinner, Christine told me she had moved to a small village in Spain after college with a job to teach English. The transition into that adventure had been more difficult than the move to Phoenix. In Spain, she had been surrounded in a new place with a different culture. She had been immersed in a language that she knew but had never been exposed to in such an all-consuming way. Yet she loved it. And she saw the adventure through. And when it was done, she moved back to her hometown of San Diego not really knowing what to do next.

But true adventurers always find a new journey and Christine fell into a new career in San Diego. When the opportunity came up to move to Phoenix, it just felt right to move. When she was invited to this event, she came alone, not knowing what to expect.

Our conversation was cut short that evening as the presentation we came for began. And at the end of it, Christine and I walked out of the theater together. She wanted to hit the restroom. I was being lured across the breezeway by the rumor of cupcakes. And so, we parted ways. I glanced over my shoulder once, watching her disappear into the crowd. She left, just as she had come, with a natural ease, as if her path had already been set and Christine was simply following it.

Sometimes life just naturally falls into place like that and the right people just magically appear. In everyone's life, we all have moments where we complain about how hard life can be…but it doesn't have to be that way. Sometimes it is nice to drift wherever the world takes us... because it is in those moments, we often receive the most wonderful gifts.

To be continued…

Some Women Can't Be Put Into A Box
Friend #21 – Jen

I'd been lured across the breezeway at the Mesa Arts Center with the promise of cupcakes. A decorated table displaying a full array of decadent cupcakes sat at the bottom of the stairway. I slowly stalked the full length of the table, eyeing the cupcakes, each one more delicious-looking than the next and finally settled on a chocolate-on-chocolate number that made me salivate. I picked it up and immediately realized how difficult it was going to be to eat a cupcake gracefully.

Strategically thinking that I needed some type of support, I meandered over to an area of tables, slowly dismembering the paper from around the bottom of the cupcake. I had no sooner taken a bite when I was suddenly sharing my table with a couple. Another couple came up right behind them. We all engaged in small talk but I was very consciously aware of the woman to my left. She was older than me, but confident and elegant in a way that I've always aspired to be.

I didn't get to talk to her much that evening as she was busy talking to the mayor, but I did find out that she is running for Mesa City Council...in my district! She was so intriguing that I took a chance and asked her if she would like to be my new friend for the week, since this is what I do now. And I was absolutely delighted when she said yes!

We met back up in a quirky little coffee shop in downtown Mesa. Jen was just as fashion-forward as I remembered. She leaned back in a retro cushioned chair and told me her first job was in fashion merchandising at Goldwater's Department store. She had quit college for that job. It had been her dream job. She hated it.

So in order to get away from the stress at Goldwater's, Jen started bass fishing. I cocked my head. Bass fishing??? It was hard to envision someone so cosmopolitan out on a lake, fishing. But Jen grew up in Arizona in a time when this city was a lot more rural than it is today. Her family had fished growing up so she had learned, too. She was spending a day on the lake when someone suggested she enter a fishing tournament where she could win money. It was just a little backwards tournament but Jen actually won the grand prize of $500. It was such easy money that Jen started entering more bass fishing tournaments. And that original $500 wasn't a fluke. Jen was good at bass fishing…well, actually she was great at it. She began winning more and more tournaments.

After a while, people began to take notice that this blonde-haired, blue-eyed, waif of a woman was winning…a lot. And once she secured her first bass fishing sponsorship, she realized it would be tight but she could live on that money for a full year. That's when she quit her job at Goldwater's and began bass fishing full time. She even landed herself on the cover of a bass fishing magazine. Some Japanese businessmen happened to be in Arizona learning about American bass fishing when they saw Jen's picture on the cover of that magazine. She stood out because she was so different than what a typical bass fisherman would look like. The Japanese businessmen were intrigued so they asked her to come to compete in two bass fishing tournaments in Japan. It was an adventure and Jen was in her late twenty's, still young enough to appreciate such things, so she accepted their invitation.

Her first tournament in Japan was at the base of Mt. Fuji. It was a tough day for her on the lake and Jen only came back with three tiny fish. She was devastated, thinking her new Japanese benefactors were going to be disappointed. As it happened, it was a tough day on the lake for everyone and Jen won the tournament! In the next tournament, she placed in the top ten. Because she had done so well, the Japanese asked her to stay in Japan for a full year.

It was exciting to be in a place so different from where she came from, so Jen stayed. She met a fantastic group of friends who were fascinated by Americana, and her, as an extension of that fascination. In fact, they liked her so much they began to ask Jen to consult on bass fishing products, and when Jen's year in Japan was up, she continued her consultations long distance. Consulting paid enough money that Jen no longer had to fish for a living. Jen's close relationship with the Japanese also led her to discover that the Japanese's obsession with precision actually meant they were manufacturing superior bass fishing lures. Jen then began manufacturing her own lures that were made in Japan. She sold them as a high-end product in American fishing shops. Everyone told her she was crazy…but her line was a huge success.

By 2009, Jen began to feel like her life had become too homogenized behind the walls of her gated community. The comings and goings were so mundane. Jen found herself craving simplicity and a fresh start so she purchased a cozy, little bungalow in downtown Mesa. In an effort to meet her neighbors, Jen created what she called "Jen's Open House". Once a month, her home was open to anyone who wanted to come, but...you had to bring something. It could be wine. Or art. Or another person. Jen's old neighbors came from their gated communities. Jen's new neighbors ambled down the street. And once a month, Jen's home became filled with art and laughter as a diverse group of people set aside their differences and gathered together as a community. It was a place where an eighty-year-old priest and a twenty-year-old tattoo artist could be found immersed in a lively discussion on any number of topics.

It was through these evenings that Jen came to love the diversity of her hometown. Her idea is that a community is only sustainable if it is diverse. Change is a constant. What is new and considered "luxury" today will not be that way forever. Overly homogenized communities tend to fall into neglect after a few decades, but if a community can continue to have enough low, middle, and high-income housing, that community will be viable for years to come. That is what she wants for Mesa. That is where she sees the future.

Part of the reason Jen is so passionate about becoming a member of the Mesa City Council is because she wants to keep the heart of Mesa beating strong, stronger than it ever has before. And as I was sitting across from her, I was so full of admiration for this beautiful, smart, conscientious woman who succeeded in a man's industry with grace, long before there was the cry of "me too". This isn't a typical politician who wants to hide behind closed doors. This is a woman who wants to fight for the people in her community and someone whose wisdom should be used to mold the foundation of the future.

It also just goes to show you that you never know who you are going to meet over the unwrapping of a simple cupcake...so you might as well just go for it.

The Mountain
Friend #22 – Antony

Having to find a date for my friend, Katie's wedding launched me right back onto the hamster wheel that we all know as online dating. To be honest, I don't agree to go out with many guys. There are just so many that you must have sorting criteria and you have no idea if you are weeding out someone you might actually get along with…or not. Either way, it hasn't been an entirely successful endeavor for me…and yet, I'm still drawn to it like a moth to a flame.

A few weeks ago, I got a message from a guy so I checked out his profile…and as I was reading through it, I started to laugh. He was a handsome guy but he was literally twice my size, solid muscle, covered in tattoos with a long black beard and gauges in his ears. The thought of this Jason Momoa-look-alike sitting next to me, the conservative-looking, tattooless girl, somehow tickled my funny bone. So much so that I actually responded back by saying, "Thanks for the laugh! We would look completely ridiculous together."

And then I immediately apologized, realizing I probably just insulted the guy. Me and my big mouth! He was kind and gracious about my misstep, but I could tell he took those words to mean that I was blowing him off. Did I mean to do that? I wasn't sure. So I slept on it and in the morning, I thought to myself, "Aren't you doing this whole one-friend-a-week thing because you want to meet people different than yourself?" So I messaged him back and we agreed to meet.

Antony showed up nicely dressed. He was doting and sweet, a complete gentleman. He asked the waiter to take a photo of us together. He talked about how he was looking for a nice girl. He said he wanted to settle down, treat someone right and have someone love him back in return. Before leaving, he added me to his social media page and casually mentioned that a lot of what was on the page was purely for image purposes...which, of course, only made me want to look. I just wasn't prepared for what I was about to see.

Antony's entire social media page was filled with images of women treated as objects. The main photograph showed him in the foreground with three scantily clad women behind him. There were lots of selfies and flexing muscles. I was also horrified to also see the photo snapped of me and him lying right in the middle of it all, like a trophy.

What the heck?!?!

He was a giant teddy bear in person but was this the image he wanted to project to the world? The man and the social media page seemed very different. I remembered a TED Talk I'd seen recently on vulnerability. It talked about how men have a difficult time being vulnerable because they don't want to be seen as weak. I wondered if this might be the case with Antony...so I went out with him again just to get a second take on the situation.

The entire night I felt like I was digging a trench around a mountain, trying to get to the core of who he was as a person. I just couldn't dig deep enough to really know. It was troubling. Again, he reiterated that he wanted to find a nice girl to settle down with...but nice girls (particularly those in their 40's), don't want to date someone who portrays themselves like that. They want a man they can proudly bring around their family, friends and coworkers.

I have found that people tend to accumulate those around them based on their own reflection, or the image they put out into to the world. If someone gives off the image that visual appearance is the most important thing then they are going to draw people into their life that cover their insecurities with plastic surgery and thrive off of drama.

Antony may have once been that guy. I think he knows he needs to change but as long as he keeps the same image, that change can never take place.

And then I had a horrible thought. What image was I reflecting onto the world to bring such a person into my life? I took a moment to really sit back and think about it. And I came up with: evolving. I am evolving. I'm not the same person I was a year ago…or even six months ago, for that matter. The habit of meeting new people has made me more confident, more curious and happier. I'm not the person I'm meant to be yet but I am enjoying the journey.

So my wish for Antony is that he can find his path because I think the one he is on, no longer suits him. I think he has a deep-seeded desire to be loved and at the end of the day, don't we all deserve that?

The Happy Lady
Friend #23 – Connie

Sometimes a girl just wants to see a movie. And sometimes, particularly if you are single, no one is available to go with you.

This was my plight a few weeks ago. So what did I do? I went by myself! Only I arrived WAY too early and found myself sitting on the bench outside the theater. The hallway was virtually empty. I tried playing on my phone but the wifi connection was bad. So I sighed, leaned back into the wall and entertained myself by watching people passing by.

I'd been sitting there for about fifteen minutes when I saw an older woman, in her seventies, coming towards me in a bright pink t-shirt that said, "Be Happy". As she was walking past the recycling bin, she read the sign aloud: "Recycle your glasses". She then moved her hand to the spectacles on her face and said, "But I like mine!"

I giggled and she smiled at me. "I know what they meant," she said.

"I know…but I would have thought that, too."

The woman walked up to where I was sitting. "I like you," she said. She reached into her pocket and said, "Here, you get a happy face."

I reached out to see what she was going to give me and she dropped a clear rock, the kind used in modern flower vases, with a happy face sticker stuck on top. As soon as the object was placed in my hand, I could feel warmth creep up my arm and suddenly I was grinning from ear to ear. I loved it! And that's how I met Connie.

Actually…that's how a lot of people meet Connie. If you live in Mesa, you may have run into her already.

But five years ago, she found she wasn't all that happy. She'd had a stroke, and in the process, broke her foot in the fall. The stroke forced her to give up her job as a teacher, which she didn't realize was a key part of her identity. The broken foot put her in a wheelchair. For a while, people would stop to help her when she was in the wheelchair but when she started getting around on her own again, she found that people were less willing to give of their time, and she became…well…depressed.

Connie started doing research on how to be happy and what she found was that happiness is a choice. Sure, there are a lot of other things that go into it. The simple act of smiling releases a chemical in the brain that causes you to be happier. Being positive is another one of traits truly happy people exhibit. But Connie also realized that a true simple connection, even a small one, can make a huge impact in people's lives. So she began handing out her happy faces wherever she went. She doesn't judge. She always asks first and mostly, people take them with a smile.

And as I was talking to her, I realized that while Connie is handing out smiley faces, I'm making new friends. They are two different styles of connecting with people…but, hopefully, they produce the same result. This experiment was started to make me feel better about my life but nowadays, all I care about is the happiness of other people. Connie said, "If you can make people happy, you can change the world." It's a bold statement. But what if she's right?

Connie often takes her dog to the dog park. One day, she was walking into the park with her dog just as she had so many times. She had only been there for a few minutes when a man approached her. He had been sitting off to the side, alone, thinking of committing suicide. He asked God to send him a sign and lifted his eyes to see Connie, coming over the hill in her 'Be Happy' t-shirt. The light caught the letters and made them glow. The man hugged her, told her she had just saved his life. She told me the story with tears brimming up in her eyes.

That's the power of being happy.

And the best part is she is not perfect. She openly admitted that there are old ruts in her brain that are so deep she has trouble redirecting those negative thoughts. When she was a child, her family believed education was wasted on girls. Girls were supposed to grow up and be good wives to their husbands. But Connie had always been smart. In fact, she was so smart that she was awarded a college scholarship that resulted in a huge debate among Connie's family members about whether or not her parents should let her go.

No one in her family had ever attended college. All of these years later, Connie remembers her parents coming into her bedroom. She vividly remembers her father telling her that they were going to let her take the scholarship and then shaking his finger at her he said, "But don't you let it make you uppity." And all her life, Connie has shunned accolades and advancement. Why? Because of her deep-seeded fear of being uppity. Well, it's actually her deep-seeded fear of disappointing her father…but that's been more than fifty years ago. The world has changed, yet the rut in her brain runs deep.

None of us is perfect. No one has happy thoughts all the time. It's actually the unhappy ones that make us human, but Connie is a true testament of what one woman can do with a little determination. She sponsors a "happy" club at Cortez High School because she once read there is an overwhelming amount of depression among high school students. She's made a difference in a lot of people's lives, one smile at a time. I can personally attest that when she dropped her "happy" rock into my hand, it made me feel special. And loved. And fortunate that I have an outlet to share with the world about one ordinary woman who has decided to make her mark on the world through the goodness and purity of simply being happy.

The Wilted
Friend #24 – Betty

A long-time friend, who is the general manager of an assisted living facility, suggested that since I was making new friends, I should come and visit some of the residents at her facility…and I thought, "What a great idea!" When I was a kid, my church group regularly visited a nursing home just up the street. Where had that habit gone? I couldn't remember. But it's been years since I've heard of anyone visiting the elderly.

It took a while to coordinate on my part but I finally found a time that would work. My friend, Amey, greeted me, took me on a tour of the facility and told me she knew just who I should meet. Eventually, she stood in the doorway of one of the rooms, introduced me to Betty and then she was gone. I walked into the dimly lit room and smiled at the woman sitting in a wheelchair. She asked me to pardon the mess. She'd just moved in. She told me that she'd apparently had a stroke.

"You mean you don't know?" I said, teasing.

She shook her head.

I asked her if she remembered it. She said no.

Betty told me that she was ninety-four-years-old and that she had been married to her husband, Stan, for seventy-two years. She met Stan when she was fourteen years old in her Iowa hometown. They married when she was nineteen because Stan was going off to the war. Normally, her parents wouldn't have agreed to let her get married so young but they knew they wouldn't be able to live with themselves if anything ever happened to Stan. Luckily, it didn't. Betty and Stan had two sons once the war was over. Stan worked in a department store. Betty started out as a cashier but eventually worked her way into an advertising job, managing the advertising for Best Western in the 1970's.

I told Betty I worked in advertising. She grinned in delight. "We have so much in common!"

I kept asking Betty questions, just like I do everyone but Betty seemed to fade between the answers, as if she were having difficulty remembering. I wondered if that stroke had caused more damage than I could see on the outside. Stan died a year ago last December. After Betty's stroke, her sons thought it best that she received round the clock care, which is how she ended up in the assisted living home. One of her sons lives in Colorado. The other lives in California. They call…but their lives are elsewhere.

As I sat looking at Betty, I realized I was witnessing a woman who had lived beyond her life. The love of her life, the man she'd grown together with like two intertwining trees, was gone. The home they built together had been swept away by her stroke. The children she raised were off raising their own. Just when Betty had reached a point in her life when she no longer desired change, her entire life was turned upside down and she found herself living in the assisted living home where I found her.

I asked her how she liked the other people in the facility. Betty said the women were very private and hard to get to know. She described one woman, Edith, who never speaks to Betty but always smiles. Betty said she remembers Edith's name because Edith was her mother's name. Once Betty told one of the nurses that Edith needed her meat cut up and Edith had looked particularly grateful. I asked Betty if, perhaps, Edith had been rendered mute because of a stroke. I could tell she hadn't considered that possibility. It may have fallen into one of those bruised places in Betty's brain.

There was silence amongst us for a while. To fill the space, I began to babble on about my own life, something I try not to do when visiting someone new, but old, nervous ticks are hard to break. At first, I didn't realize what was happening, but my words poured over Betty like water bringing a wilted plant back to life. It was then that I realized that Betty didn't need to recount her own story. She'd done that for ninety-four years. She was tired of that story. The story that mattered to her…was mine.

The charades of my own life brought animation to the dimly lit room and when I left, I knew I'd done a good deed. Sometimes, life brings all of us moments when we feel down and the best way to escape those negative thoughts is to focus on happier ones. There aren't a lot of happy thoughts in Betty's life right now. The kindest thing I could do was to give her some of mine. And so I did.

The Beloved
Friend #25 – Mary

Mary grew up as the only girl in a household with five boys. She was largely sheltered as a child. So when she was of the age to go to college, she wanted to break out and spread her wings. That's why she left her home in New York to attend Arizona State University. It was far enough away that she felt like she was on her own but she did have a brother who was also attending ASU, just in case she ever needed anything. She never did.

Once when she was home on summer break, she was with a friend at local hangout when the most handsome man she'd ever seen came up to talk to her. He was 6'4" and gorgeous. He also lived in the area. They went on a date the next night and continued the relationship even when she went back to ASU. She was wild about him! They talked about a future together, getting married. And then, he missed a phone call he normally would have made. At first, Mary made excuses for him. He was in the military and sometimes missions come up unexpectedly…but his absence stretched out and Mary didn't hear from him. She tried to contact him on multiple occasions but her inquiries always went unanswered.

Then, one day, he finally called. She asked him where he had been. He made excuses, but he still said he loved her. They made plans to see each other the next time Mary was in New York. And that was the last time Mary ever heard from him.

Mary called his parent's house to try to reach him the next time she was in New York to visit. His father picked up the phone and when she asked to speak with him, his father said, "Mary, don't you know? He's married."

Later, she wondered if she should have asked more details but the shock of hearing the words forced her to get off the phone quickly. She never knew what happened to that guy. All the love and hurt she had for him, she wrapped up in a little box and moved it into a far corner of her soul so she would never have to think about it. But every now and then, she would wonder what happened. She wondered what she had done wrong.

Mary stayed in Arizona to teach when she graduated. She never married, never had children and instead poured all of her efforts into her teaching career. And then the magic of social media came into all of our lives…and Mary found him.

They began chatting online. He had been married and divorced twice. Mary asked him what had happened all those years ago. He claimed he had loved her but that she'd told him she'd never move back to New York. Mary was aghast. She had no recollection of ever having a conversation of that nature! She knew in her heart that she would have moved back for him. And he confirmed what Mary had long suspected. While Mary was away at ASU, he had found a local girl that he had gotten pregnant. Apparently, the last call he'd made to Mary was on the night before his wedding. He was calling to tell her he was getting married…but lost his nerve, leaving Mary to wonder for decades what she'd done wrong.

It was only one moment in a lifetime of moments, yet the emotional impact was like a bomb.

That isn't to say that love has never been in her life. Mary has always had a passion for teaching and people and adventure. She's lived a full passionate life. One of her favorite quotes is from the first few moments of the movie, "Love Actually" that says: "Whenever I get gloomy with the state of the world, I think about the arrivals gate at Heathrow Airport. General opinion's starting to make out that we live in a world of hatred and greed, but I don't see that. It seems to me that love is everywhere. Often, it's not particularly dignified or newsworthy, but it's always there – fathers and sons, mothers and daughters, husbands and wives, boyfriends, girlfriends, old friends. When the planes hit the Twin Towers, as far as I know none of the phone calls from the people on board were messages of hate or revenge – they were all messages of love. If you look for it, I've got a sneaky feeling you'll find that love actually is all around."

And everyone loves Mary.

Next March, Mary will retire from teaching and a new chapter in her life will begin. She still plans on being an advocate for teachers and living her life to the fullest. I'm sure she will sneak in a traveling adventure or two. And maybe now that Mary knows what happened all those years ago. Maybe new doors filled with love will open in Mary's life because the one thing I know for sure is that passionate people always find passion in their lives somewhere.

Standing Amidst the Waves
Friend #26 – Mitch

Do you affect the world? Or does the world affect you?

Last Saturday, Big Brothers, Big Sisters of Arizona hosted a LGBTQ Awareness seminar. Since I'm a Big Sister, I was invited. I'm not entirely sure what I was expecting but when I arrived, the majority of the attendees were men.

At the very beginning of the seminar, a man behind me asked, "Isn't this all just a choice?" I could immediately feel tensions rise around the room like an earthquake. The facilitators and the audience had a lot to say, but there was one man at the far end of the table where I was sitting who calmly waited until everyone else said their peace.

When, finally, he was called on to speak, he turned to the man behind me and said, "I am biracial. So in school when they passed out forms for you to check a box beside your ethnicity, I could neither check the box that said 'white' nor the box that said 'black' without denying some part of myself. These people are just asking for a box to check. That's all. It doesn't matter whether you understand it or not. Just give them a box." Boom. The matter was settled.

And that's how I met Mitch.

His parents met in 1977 while working in an assisted living facility in Compton, California and while there was a lot of love, it wasn't an easy childhood. Mitch remembers a road trip his family took to see family in Louisiana. As they drove through Texas, Mitch's father had his wife lie all the way back in the passenger seat with a coat covering her face because in those days if a black man was caught with a white woman in certain parts of Texas, the man was beaten and the woman was raped. Even Mitch's best friends in Compton sometimes called him "honky". And there were lots of instances when Mitch felt like he didn't fit anywhere. In those days there were no boxes for him. It could have made a lesser person bitter.

But when Mitch was twenty, he bought his first house and as soon as he moved in, he discovered there was a water leak under the foundation. The company that came out to assess the damage told him it was going to cost three thousand dollars to fix it. That was three thousand dollars that Mitch didn't have. He immediately went into his bedroom and cried. And then he got up, went out to rent a jackhammer, dug up the foundation and taught himself how to lay the pipe. When it was done, he knew there was nothing in his life he couldn't do. And he's lived that way ever since.

Mitch is 6'3", bald, with tattoos and piercings. On the outside, he looks like an intimidating dude but on the inside, he's kind, respectful, and self-aware with a quiet confidence that commands the room. Kids and animals gravitate towards him. He's slow to anger but when he does it's scathing.

Once, one of his employees did something stupid at work and he lost his temper. He stormed back to his office, realized what he had done and asked his assistant manager to bring the employee in. The employee, scared he was about to lose his job, immediately began gushing an apology. Mitch held up his hand and said, "Stop. You have nothing to apologize for. You made a mistake but I'm the one that owes you the apology. I shouldn't have lost my temper and called you out amidst your peers."

And that's the take control kind of guy he is. He's a gun enthusiast but not because he wants to maim. It's the ability to control something out of control that is the draw for him. If life were the ocean and the waves were insecurity, fear, indecision and anger, how many of us would have the strength to stand steadfast instead of being swept off our feet? Yet that's the type of man Mitch is. He lives his life with quiet strength and when the waves grow strong, he finds a way to hold the them back for both himself and the people he loves.

The Actress
Friend #27 – Debbie

Confession: I've always wanted to be an actress. I think it
started in the high school drama club, the endorphins you get
performing in front of a crowd that is fixated on your every
movement and emotion. I wasn't particularly good at it. I
have a difficult time controlling my eyes and facial
movements that react honestly, in the moment and often can't
be duplicated. But I am fascinated by those who have that
gift.

So when a friend suggested I sit down with a real life actress,
I leapt at the opportunity. There were so many questions I
had about people who live their lives portraying others. I'd
always had a notion that great actors must have, at some point
in their lives, developed a skill for putting on a façade in their
real life in order to escape that reality. Debbie told me that
wasn't really the case. Great acting is about putting on a coat
of someone else's back story to wear during the duration of
the performance. Because of this, actors need to have a great
deal of empathy. They need to feel for others as if they were
feeling the emotion, themselves. Debbie believes this is why
the LGBTQ community has been so accepted into the
theater. It's the nature of their jobs to provide empathy to all
people regardless of their orientation.

And Debbie should know. She has been in the theater world
for a long time. Over the past thirty years she has worked for
Childsplay, a local theater that puts on family friendly shows

in Tempe, Arizona. Because of her age, she has most recently been delegated to more directorial duties, claiming she is too old to be the starlet. Well…maybe…but you can still see the vitality in Debbie's cheeks, the passion in her eyes, the warmth in her voice. I asked if she ever wanted to pursue her craft in Los Angeles, figuring there must be loads of opportunity there, but Debbie just laughed. She claimed she was too short and curvy for what LA wanted…but she also never had aspirations to act commercially. The stage has always been the love of her life.

She was married once for seven years. He was a nice man and at first, he loved how passionately she felt about the theater. He was the type of man who would help her with sets and behind-the-scenes work, but eventually he grew jealous of Debbie's first love. Debbie believes her marriage was a sacrifice she gave up for feminism, as many women of her generation did. The feminists taught the young girls to believe they could do anything but the young men still wanted nurturing women like their mothers. Debbie couldn't deny the feminist part of herself…so she chose the stage.

As we talked, the mental pedestal I had placed the actress on began to subside. The light coming through the window caressed the soft lines of her face, making them more distinct and the actress on the pedestal became more real.

We both went to Western Kentucky University. Debbie was a few years ahead of me but at the time she was attending, Western had one of the most prestigious drama departments in the nation. She got her masters at Arizona State University and then the desert just stuck, much like it did for me. She said her mother should have been an actress but there wasn't a lot of opportunity for acting where Debbie grew up in Memphis. So Debbie's mother sang, instead. Debbie has one brother who is a writer and shares the creative passion of telling a good story that she does. She has another brother and sister that chose more scientific paths. It was a creative family but not so different from the family I grew up in.

And you would think as an actress, Debbie would crave the spotlight as if it were a bit of espresso injected directly into her veins. It is the passion that drives her but not necessarily the thing that energizes her. Instead, Debbie admits she is a bit of introvert finding rejuvenation within the quiet moments as she is gardening at home or spending time with her two cats. It's as if the creative energy that drives her bursts forth so dynamically from a person who is so magnificently ordinary in so many ways.

Of course, if you were sitting next to her in a restaurant, you might be captivated by her stories or her ability to be animated. Debbie seems to always carry the art of the dramatic around with her like a prized handbag, but by the end of the conversation, we were reduced to comparing notes about the changes at the university we both shared like two old friends. And I'd like to think we had become friends as the mysterious aura of "actress" faded into the reality of two women who simply had a lot in common. She tells her stories on the stage. I tell my stories on the page. Yet within those differences, there is a lot of the same.

The Unifier
Friend #28 – Fred

In celebration of making twenty-six new friends in six months, I decided to release a video on social media that a local news station had produced back in January featuring my '52 new friends' project. As I expected, I received messages from people who wanted to stick their hands up in support of the project. Fred was one of the first to jump on board.

I met him in a quaint little coffee shop in downtown Gilbert. The shop, itself, was small but just outside was a yard full of mismatched seating and greenery. It reminded me a bit of the time I had spent in Portland, Oregon. And Fred seemed to blend right in with his walking shorts and his t-shirt featuring a local band. We ordered our coffee and found a seat with some shade, in front of the misters. It was still early in the day but certainly warm, as Arizona mornings tend to be. Fred grew up in Vancouver, Washington, which is just on the other side of Portland making the ambiance of the coffee shop even more relevant.

Fred carried himself with a calm confidence, chest up, back straight as he sipped his coffee. He's spent the last fifteen years of his retirement working at REI. I'm sure the outdoor equipment and discounts initially lured him in but he's stayed there because of the people. He loves asking customers about their next hiking adventure. Sometimes, the hike might be local like Bright Angel Trail or sometimes, it might be exotic like Madagascar. Every customer has a different experience to share.

I asked Fred what type of job he retired from and he calmly said he used to be a police officer. I blinked twice. Immediately, my brain leapt to a video I'd seen of Mesa police officers beating a man and then my brain took a second leap to a car chase I saw on the show 'Cops' the night before. Both of those images were threatening and filled with angst, which was much different from the serene man I saw sitting across from me, mildly sipping his coffee.

Fred fell into law enforcement by way of accident. One of his buddies from the military, wanted to go check it out and Fred, who had a wife and baby, at the time, to support, decided to tag along. His buddy left the police academy after a month but Fred stayed on. He liked the potential for excitement but mostly, he liked the people. So much of what we see on the news nowadays is the police versus ordinary citizens. Fred's demeanor made me think back to old images of a cherub-faced, friendly, local policeman who stopped to play kickball with the local kids. Once upon a time, a police officer conjured up the image of role model, not something to be feared. Where have those days gone? Has the world changed? Or has our perception of our world changed?

Since Fred retired, he likes to travel. He said in Thailand all the people are smiling. He said the Kingdom of Bhutan measures their government's effectiveness by the happiness of its people. And how are we faring in the United States? Lately, we seem more divided than ever.

There was a man who worked on the police force with Fred for many years. They were, of course, friends. Fred never knew the man's political affiliation until the advent of social media. Only through the internet did Fred discover how different their politics were. Fred also had another friend he always slipped a 'friends and family' coupon to during a particular time of year, but this year, the friend declined the discount because of REI's stance on firearms. It's all well and good to have strong beliefs on topics, but not at the expense of all else. Not when it's dividing us away from one another in ways we can't repair.

What really matters is the connection we have as a society to each other. No matter what a person's spiritual or political beliefs are, I believe the great majority of people don't wish other people harm and want a better world. We all have differing opinions on how to get to a better world or what exactly that looks like, but at our core essence, we are much more similar than we are different. The one thing this experiment has taught me is that every person I sit down with is unique and special, no matter how different I, at first, think we are.

I believe Fred sought me out because first and foremost, this experiment is about connection. And maybe we need more connections in our lives. Fred didn't know it, but I was having a difficult time that morning. Someone I deeply cared about was going into surgery that afternoon. I was also having my typical problems with some man who had wandered into my life, and I was so upset I'd worked myself up into an emotional cocoon. Sitting with Fred, talking and sipping our caffeinated beverages surrounded by lush natural shrubbery, I felt the weight temporarily fall from my shoulders. I felt myself opening to another human being and I felt a connected calm, a gift to me from Fred.

I would like to say I was the one with the most giving power in the construct of this experiment but in reality, I'm getting back just as much as I give.

The Unnoticed
Friend #29 – Ashton

Ashton is a twin. The pair couldn't be more identical. In fact, they are so identical one twin usually doesn't survive. The babies were taken from their mother's womb at thirty-two weeks and the only differences between the two are the hormonal ones after birth…yet Ashton's sister always knew there was something different about Ashton.

Ashton knew it too.

The pair had a cookie-cutter childhood in Ahwatukee, Arizona, where the homes were new and the neighborhoods were filled with white, middle-class families. The twins were honor students. They went to church every Sunday. Ashton had a particular affinity for art.

The twins chose to go to a Christian college in Spokane, Washington and it was during those years where this story gets really interesting. Ashton's sister identifies as a lesbian woman. Ashton identifies as non-binary, which means that on a gender line where male is on one side and female is on the other, Ashton falls somewhere in the gray in between.

Ashton might be that person that your child once pointed to in public and said, "Mommy, is that a man or a woman?" really loudly, the person you didn't really notice because you were so busy trying to hush-up the child that you overlooked them. But if you'd taken a moment to really see the person in front of you…Ashton is beautiful… with shining eyes, soft skin and a smile that lights up the room. There is an internal joy that emanates out of their* mouth into words intelligent beyond their years. And the unsure looks, the hushed questions beyond their back, those are all daggers to the soul.

Think you've never met a transgender person? Ashton told me that conservatively there are at least thirty thousand people living in Arizona who are transgender. That means you have crossed paths with someone who is transgender. Did you notice them? Ashton pointed out that the coffee shop I had picked at random contained at least two transgender people, not including Ashton, while we were sitting there.

Ashton came out in college, which was no easy task in at a conservative university. At the beginning of their freshmen year, there were no openly transgender people on campus but at the end of their senior year, there were a few who were no longer hiding in dark corners, hoping to go unnoticed. Ashton felt like they had changed the stigma there and put their passion for art on hold in order to work on transgender legislation in Arizona. It was just too important, because a transgender person's body often doesn't match how they feel on the inside and they live in constant fear that their medical rights will be taken away.

For example, Ashton worries that one day they will be denied gynecological care because their driver's license says they are male. Think about that for a moment. As I sat across from this gentle soul, a cold, prickly hand reached into my chest and squeezed my heart. That fear is real and legitimate. For years, Ashton had to walk around with their breasts bound under three layers to feel normal, even in the blistering one hundred-fifteen degree Arizona summers. An unexpected automobile breakdown could throw them into heatstroke with so many layers. Removing breast tissue is considered cosmetic, is not covered by most insurance and is expensive.

Ashton said in some ways they miss the bliss and naivety of their cookie-cutter Ahwatukee neighborhood. There is something to be said for being ignorant to the evils of the world. And the transgender community has a lot to be angry about. They are angry because they live in a constant state of fear of being judged and misunderstood. They are NOT monsters or deviants or child molesters. They are simply people who are trying to laugh and love and live out their own personal truth, just like every other human being on this planet.

*Dear Grammar Nazis, Ashton uses the pronouns 'they' and 'them' so in order to be sensitive, I am using those pronouns throughout this piece.

An Enjoyable Life
Friend #30 – Mark

One of the joys of Mark's life is the high-rise condo he owns overlooking Tempe Town Lake. It's a small, one-bedroom dwelling with clean lines, unbefitting to any clutter. The building residents are friendly and familiar, making the tower a community. The views are incredible, and if Mark leaves for an international traveling adventure, the space is virtually unchanged from the moment he closes the door to the moment he returns. Mark loves the simplicity it gives his life. It is his sanctuary.

And for Mark, he finds genius in simplicity. He likes to walk places when he has the opportunity. He loves riding his bike and dining in quaint, local restaurants. He loves music and cars. A sticker to put on his wheels might be the thing that brings him an enormous amount of joy that day. And he does feel a lot of joy in his life. His motto is "Enjoy Life Daily" and often, he does. Of course, no one can be joyful all the time. There was a period last year when he broke things off with his fiancé that life became more difficult, but he always makes the attempt. And he confesses that we all need challenging times in our lives. It makes us appreciate when things are good.

Mark's passion is in helping people. He started his personal coaching business in 2011 and every time he gets a note, thanking him for his help and encouragement in making someone a success, Mark's heart grows just a little bit in his chest. He's proud of the person for taking the steps necessary to accomplish their goals and he is grateful for the wisdom the Lord has given him to help others help themselves. Over the past few years, Mark has become exceptionally close with the members of his men's prayer group and even goes so far as to say that the group has a bond of unconditional love flowing between them. He even credits the group with helping him to grow his own personal faith.

He's smart, handsome and well-read. He has a wealth of knowledge on a number of topics but he's also a great listener. In fact, he's such a good listener that it's difficult for a babbler-mouth like me to get to know the man beneath his confident, balanced exterior. He exudes kindness and genuineness. He's a person that likes to reach out and give a stranger a compliment, even if they give him a look of shock…because strangers don't really reach out without intention anymore. But Mark does.

To look at him and his life, one would think Mark has always been blessed as one of the lucky ones. But buried underneath years of gratitude and happiness is a reality that the occasional onlooker doesn't see. When Mark was in college, he suffered from depression. So much so that he eventually sought help because he was contemplating taking his own life. He didn't know it then because he was so young but happiness doesn't always come in a straight line. There are moments in life when we all feel hopeless. But then the moment passes…and life goes on.

Recently, Mark has taken the time to celebrate his victory in overcoming that period of his life. It makes him even more grateful now for every day he has and he wants to share his story because somewhere out there a person is suffering from depression. They are thinking of committing suicide and Mark is the living example of how beautiful a life can become if life is simply allowed to grow.

The Artist
Friend #31 – Brandon

Brandon is onto something big. He can feel it in his bones…as if his dreams are finally coming to fruition.

He is an artist, a multimedia body artist. What is that? We met through friends so before our meeting, Brandon sent me an extraordinary image of a person dressed as a demigod, who seemed like they would fit in the Marvel universe. But the image was remarkably life-like, as if they had walked out of a movie. My first reaction was that it was cool, but I thought it to be rather large to be tattooed on someone. That shows you how much I know! The image Brandon sent me was of an actual person Brandon had visually transformed through the use of body paint and other elements you'd find at a craft shop. He then poses his models and photographs them to create works of art that are simply amazing.

He's always been a creator. In fact, at this point in his life, he is more comfortable creating than not creating. He never wants to retire. And he's worked in virtually every medium: drawing, painting, sculpting, acting, modeling, video production, photography. If you can think it, Brandon has probably done it. He is an artist in every sense of the word. But for much of his life, he has been the quintessential starving artist, just waiting for his big break…and he's learned a lot of lessons along the way.

For eighteen years, Brandon worked in IT. It was hard to picture him hiding his talent behind a computer screen as he sat next to me, gracefully draped onto the chair, sipping chai tea with a sparkly silver scarf wrapped around his neck. His IT job paid the bills while he honed his craft. He quit his job once to become a full-time artist but eventually, had to go back to work. He felt like failure...yet it wasn't in his nature to stop creating so he persisted. And he began working smarter.

Building his following on social media was a no brainer. I think everyone does that, but Brandon took things a step further. He found a website called patreon.com that allows regular people to sponsor artists via a monthly donation. No longer do you have to be wealthy to sponsor art. Patreon gives the masses the ability to financially sponsor beauty in the world. Brandon used this site to build an income for himself so that he could eventually become a full-time artist once again. It didn't happen overnight. It was a long, tedious process but it does give him a way to feel more financially secure and concentrate on the projects that mean the most to him.

Brandon has also grown his popularity so when Brandon announces a project, he has people applying to be his muse. That way the artwork is commissioned through them for what I think is a nominal fee...and Brandon doesn't have to worry about not getting paid. Everything is paid for in advance. He has literally created a paying market for his own art. So now, when he publishes a book of portraits, the profits from the book is the financial cherry on top, instead of a black hole of debt. I think it is brilliant marketing at its finest.

And his art is in demand. Who wouldn't want him to paint and photograph them? It is a one-of-a-kind experience! And even his books receive accolades. One fan had a book shipped to Singapore because the buyer, who lived in Vietnam, knew that if Vietnamese officials opened the book and saw the nudity, it would be immediately banned and not allowed into the country. By shipping it to Singapore, he could smuggle it in by driving it over the border. That's the type of devotion that Brandon's work brings out in people. Brandon giggled thinking about his work as contraband.

And Brandon, himself, is non-stop. Because his medium involves people, he doesn't have the luxury of having a block in creativity. He must be spontaneously brilliant at all times because that's what his customers expect…and so that is what he delivers. Sure, there are moments he's painting someone in a bar and a drunken patron sticks their fingers in his fresh paint. He still has moments where he feels underappreciated…but that just makes him human.

His life today seems like a pipe dream, a figment of the imagination, from where he started, the shy, effeminate boy who was often bullied in school. But today, Brandon is confident and courageous. And he's winning at his dream simply because through all the hardship, he persisted…and he's come out on top.

If you would like to see Brandon's work, go to www.brandonmcgill.com. There is nudity…but it's awesome!

The Soulmate

Friend #32 – Isaac

When Isaac was in college, a friend mentioned that they had another friend who attended the same university. "You should meet up," Dez said, in passing. Of course, this was before the advent of Facebook so the introduction was conducted via myspace.

In the grand scheme of things, it should have been an insignificant meeting, a moment hardly worth mentioning in a life full of moments. But Isaac and Amber had a remarkable number of things in common. They had quite a few mutual friends and their lives in Florida seemed to have just missed each other right up to the point of their first interaction. It was natural. It was easy. And Isaac and Amber fell deeply in love.

But as time went on, feelings Isaac always had pushed down deep began to surface. You see, when Isaac and Amber met, Isaac identified as a gay woman. After college, Isaac began the process of transitioning into living as a man. Amber and Isaac, who had made a career in social work, found themselves living in a small town in Texas. Mostly, the transitioning process was easy, although the judge, who approved Isaac's name change, was less than enthusiastic. "How are you working in the prisons?" he bellowed from his pedestal. Isaac wanted to say, "Well...I'm not running around naked." Instead, he said, "I'm just like everyone else." The judge simmered but eventually approved

the name change…and Isaac never had to worry about seeing
him again.

Getting the sex changed on his driver's license in a small
town was a much simpler process. When the DMV issued
Isaac's license with his new name, they mistakenly also
changed the sex on the document to male. Wanting to make
sure he was doing the right thing, Isaac went back to the
DMV. He brought in a copy of his birth certificate and
pointed out the DMV's mistake which was met with an
unwavering gaze. "You look like a boy," the government
worker said. "Your driver's license says you are a boy. So if
you want me to change this, you're gonna have to prove
otherwise." Isaac just nodded in amazement and left with a
driver's license identifying him exactly as he wanted to be
identified.

And through all this transition, Amber was there holding
Isaac's hand.

When they moved to Arizona, Isaac found a job as a social
worker. He really wanted to help people, particularly
wayward teens, but he found the system to be stifling. The
accountability system which was once set up to make the
system efficient, Isaac found to be more of a hindrance. His
entire day had to be broken down based on a certain number
of units of time…but units couldn't be combined. For
example, if he was transporting a teen from one location to
another and there was an important conversation in the car,
that unit could only be used for transportation. Yet saying the
conversation was separate, was also against the rules. And
NOT recording a conversation was also wrong. Isaac found
the system cumbersome and lacking in the fluidity needed to
actually help people.

So when another opportunity came up to work in community
education on LGBTQ issues, Isaac quit his job in social work
before he even knew he had the other job. It's the only time

in his life he's ever done something so reckless. But he was so miserable at his job as a social worker that he knew he couldn't stay. He couldn't take one more minute of it. He talked it over with Amber and in the end, she just wanted to see him happy…even though she knew if Isaac didn't immediately get the other job, financially they were going to be in trouble. Luckily, Isaac did get the job, which now gives him a tremendous amount of freedom. And he now gets to do what he does best.

Four years ago, Isaac made another big decision. He decided to ask Amber to marry him. Their mutual computer almost blew it for him with all the retargeting engagement ring ads that began popping up after Isaac did some searches…but marrying Amber was the best decision he ever made. As I listened to Isaac tell his story, I almost fell in love with Amber, myself. It's rare in this world to find a counterpart who loves so unconditionally. I imagine her as lovely, giving and deeply caring. And after thirteen years together and lots of ups and downs, Isaac and Amber's relationship is just as strong as it always has been, proving that at the end of the day, when the right two souls meet, love really does win.

The Biggest Heart
Friend #33 – Nancy

Four months ago, Nancy got laid off from her job.

She had been dealing with an abnormal mammogram for months and finally had surgery to remove her lymph nodes to solve the problem. Her boss called her two days after her surgery to let her know that she had been let go.

Nancy had spent years at that company working as a recruiter in the financial industry, ensuring new recruits that it was a great company to work for, yet all the while knowing that those who were rude, malicious and back-stabbing where the ones who were most likely to get promoted. It was a toxic environment. Nancy admitted she probably should have left long ago.

Over the past few years, changes in the financial industry had caused lay-offs at her company. Only they weren't massive layoffs that caused hysteria. It was sneaky. Once, Nancy talked to Fred on Monday and by Thursday she was getting bounce back emails. The layoffs were seemingly random. They even took those who were good at their jobs and those with massive, impeccable amounts of experience. So it wasn't a complete surprise that Nancy was laid off. It was upsetting that it occurred while Nancy was lying in bed, two days out of surgery and feeling most vulnerable. It was also upsetting because now she doesn't have the steady medical insurance she once had. It was as if everything stable had the carpet ripped right out from under it.

So Nancy found solace in the thing that has always brought her peace: dogs. She is part of that five percent of people who don't just love animals. She has been fostering them for rescue groups for as long as she can remember. And like a lot of other animal advocates, pit bulls are one of those breeds that pull on her heart strings. In fact, she once volunteered to foster a pit bull, fell in love with her and then the organization that had pulled the dog from the shelter mysteriously disappeared. So Nancy kept the dog and has loved her for years...even though the dog has caused havoc with parts of Nancy's life.

For the past nine years, Nancy has been seeing someone on and off. At one point, Nancy's boyfriend moved in with her and her pit bull...and that's when things began to go sour. For reasons Nancy can't fathom, her boyfriend has decided that pit bulls are dangerous and there is no moving him from that position. In the end, it finally came down to the boyfriend or the dog. Nancy didn't want to make the decision. In her heart, she realized that people should come before animals. But she isn't just a regular animal lover. She is one of those people that go above and beyond. It's what she loves to do. And she finally decided that anyone who truly loves her wouldn't ask her to give up something she loved so much.

So the boyfriend moved out.

Right now, Nancy is in a state of transition. I'm excited for her! She's seems less excited. Lol. But it's likely just the fear of the unknown.

For a lot of years, I think Nancy has lived in an emotional purgatory where things haven't been so bad that it would cause her to let them go…but they haven't been so good that it has brought her the happiness and joy she deserved either. I think a lot of us settle for mediocre things in our lives. I know I certainly have. Sometimes, there has to be a shake up: a breakup, a loss of a job, a health issue or something big that causes us to step back and re-evaluate our lives and what makes us happy.

I think Nancy is in that place. I just want her to laugh more. I want her to smile. I want her to find other things in her life that she can love as much as the dogs she fosters. I've spent a lot of time with those in the rescue community and one thing I've noticed is that those that rescue often treat the animals in their care like the innocent part of themselves that has once been hurt or rejected. I don't know if this is the case with Nancy or not, but I do know that anyone with a heart as large as hers deserves more respect and happiness than she's been given.

The Excuseless
Friend #34 – Rachel

I met Rachel through a sorority sister. We agreed to have our first meeting at a coffee shop late one afternoon. Five minutes before I arrived, Rachel called to say that the coffee shop was getting ready to close. Rachel, who lives downtown, had walked there so I pulled up alongside the curb and Rachel jumped in my car, ready to look for another location.

"Didn't your mama ever tell you not to get in the car with strangers?" I teased.

"You aren't a stranger. We're sisters."

And that's just how trusting Rachel is. She is a sensitive soul, a 6'1" blond Amazon. She doesn't drive because when she was fifteen, she watched a friend get hit by car. She's been afraid to operate a vehicle ever since. If she needs to go anywhere of any distance, she calls a Lyft or an Uber so she's used to jumping into strange people's cars. I wasn't even the first strange car she'd jumped into that day!

Part of the reason Rachel may be so trusting is because she is learning disabled. Technically, she has not just one, but four learning disabilities. That means a lot of things get easily jumbled up in her brain before she can take it all in, yet if you met her, you'd have no clue of the daily difficulties she faces. Her learning difficulties made school and learning extremely difficult, but Rachel has never made excuses. She has simply marched forward learning small lessons as she goes along.

When she was sixteen, Rachel's mother and father shipped her off to a boarding school in Connecticut that specialized in helping children with learning disabilities. The family was living in Hawaii at the time. I can't even begin to imagine how emotionally difficult that must have been for both Rachel and her parents…but in retrospect, Rachel said it was one of the best things her family could have done for her. Being surrounded by other children who have difficulties in learning showed Rachel that she wasn't different, that she was unique. And the school taught them all special tools to learn that make it easier to live in a world where no one thinks to accommodate those who have difficulty learning.

In Rachel's family, college was the expectation so there was an expectation that Rachel would go, whether she had a disability or not. Originally, she chose a school in Virginia but needed to take a break after a while because she was suffering from anxiety and depression, stemming not from her disability, but because colleges are a breeding ground for sexual misconduct. Rachel has had men touch her without her permission on at least five separate occasions.

Whether Rachel is aware of it or not, she exudes an energy which feels like vulnerability. Now let's be clear, Rachel is not helpless. She has learned to confront men that cat-call her. Part of me wonders if the thing I sense is not really vulnerability at all but the sweet innocence someone with learning difficulties seems to possess. At any rate, I wonder if men feel the same energy. I wonder if it draws in those with scrupulous intentions. The nurturer in me wanted to reach out and protect her because when Rachel feels emotions, she feels them deeply.

She once went on a service trip to New Orleans to work in the food kitchens down there. It was a trip that changed her life. At one food kitchen, those in need could only take the food they could put in a crate. Rachel was working the end of the line so she saw people having to make agonizing split-second decisions on whether they could take flour or sugar that week, knowing they couldn't take both. And still, Rachel's job was to hurry them along like cattle, as if their plight wasn't whether or not they would be hungry the following week. At one point, an old man, who had his crate stacked up impossibly high, tripped and fell. The contents in his crate came spilling out onto the floor. Rachel wanted to help him but she was told to stay away, that if she left her post people would steal the food they had left. So she stood there with tears in her eyes, wanting to do more, knowing she wasn't allowed to help.

That trip changed Rachel. It made her more grateful for all the things in her life.

And Rachel has wonderful things in her life, too. When she was volunteering at a local animal shelter, Rachel met a man working as a vet tech. They fell in love…and now they share an apartment and two little dogs. Last spring, Rachel graduated from ASU and miraculously found a job working in a center to help those with learning disabilities go on to higher education…just like she did.

But the most remarkable thing about Rachel is that she doesn't fully realize there is anything remarkable about her. On the day we met up, she was just coming from a doctor's appointment because over the last few months she's been suffering from crippling vertigo…yet she still showed up because she'd made a commitment to me, a stranger. How many of us make excuses to not do things we know we should? Rachel has had so many excuses to not succeed but every day she puts one step in front of the other and moves forward. I sat across from her really in awe of this beautiful, young woman. What could we do in this world if we all adopted her can-do attitude? The world would be a very different place.

The Flavorful
Friend #35 – Gordon

I was walking into my favorite martini bar to meet a new friend when I got a text saying the woman wasn't going to be able to make it because of a family emergency. I was bummed. Normally I might have turned around and left. But this was my favorite martini place... I figured one martini wasn't going to hurt anyone so I took a seat at the bar and buried my face in my phone.

After a while, I heard a soft voice behind me say, "Is anyone sitting here?"

I looked up to see an older black man pointing at the seat to my left. A quick assessment of the bar made me realize the only two empty seats were on either side of me.

"No, the seat is yours," I declared. "In fact, if you are meeting someone, I'd be happy to move down one."

Gordon shook his head and told me he was by himself so I took the cue and put my phone away. Would I have done that if I wasn't on a mission to make friends this year? I'm not sure.

Gordon told grew up in Oakland, California. His mother was an alcoholic. He never knew his father. It was just after World War II and back in those days, if you were a person of color, equality was a distant dream. Gordon remembers back during times when a person wasn't allowed north of Van Buren in Phoenix if they were black or Hispanic. That was a shocking to me! But it has to be true because he quickly Googled an article on his phone and there was the history laid out in black and white.

Gordon spent over forty years in the IT industry. I asked him how he got his start. Honestly, the story somehow got mixed in with my martini but the gist is that he had a buddy who told him there was a pig farmer in Australia, who was being subsidized to bring on personnel and train them in the IT industry. I guess the guy had other businesses other than pig farming. But since the farmer was from Australia, he didn't care about the color of a person's skin just as long as he got his money. Gordon and his buddy both went through the training program. Gordon's buddy dropped out, but Gordon made a life out of it.

And he hates social media. In the 1960's, Gordon worked for a bank that was already linking people via their relationships to approve them for loans...and that was in the 1960's! Today, Gordon says that if a person wanted to, they could find any personal information they wanted with a few flicks of their finger. Social media just makes everything more convenient to link together, your entire life mapped out on a screen.

In fact, he lived his entire life on the other side of that computer screen until he finally retired a year ago. "No one tells you what happens when you age," he said taking a sip of his cocktail. He stared into the glass longingly and confessed everyone he knew in Phoenix was still working. He now fills his days watching Maury, a show he didn't even know existed until he was banished from his career. Most of the people he knows still live in Oakland, but the cost of living keeps him from being able to return. "No one makes friends after fifty," he said. Unfortunately, based on what I have seen, he may be largely right.

So Gordon fills his weekends trying out the best restaurants Phoenix and Scottsdale have to offer. He has a list in his phone of the ones he particularly likes. Some of them I knew. Some of them I'd like to try. But as I sat on the bar stool next to him, I realized the most well-seasoned and flavor-filled thing in the entire restaurant was the older man who often sat at the bar on Saturday nights alone.

Not once did I feel like he was hitting on me. Not once did I feel threatened. We were just two strangers enjoying each other's company on a night otherwise empty for us both.

The Lightening Rod
Friend #36 – Megan

Some personalities are just too big to capture on a page…but I'm going to try.

Megan grew up in Finley, Ohio. Her first title was 'Ted and Fritzy's daughter'. It was her father that instilled in her the desire to help others. Ted participated in the Big Brother program. He was well-known, well-liked and did a lot for the small community Megan grew up in, a town that largely remains unchanged from what Megan remembers growing up.

But Megan's personality is a lightning rod for the unusual. When she was eighteen-years-old, she moved to Phoenix for the first time with her boyfriend. You know…that thing you aren't supposed to do? That time her visit to Phoenix was short-lived. Her boyfriend got hooked on meth. Life quickly eroded into a big mess so Megan packed her bags and moved back to Ohio where she tried other paths.

She trained in theatre for a while but realized she didn't like the criticism of her weight and physical appearance…so she moved on. She studied in the Methodist seminary for a period of time where she met a number of transgender ministers... (Fascinating!) …but decided that wasn't her calling. Eventually, she got married to a prominent tattoo artist in the area, which is where she picked up her second title: Her husband's wife. They were married for twelve years. In the early years, there was a lot of hard partying but eventually, reality hit them in the face. They got sober together, which you'd think would bring them closer. Unfortunately, Megan got sober. Her husband just stopped drinking. Work became his next drug of choice.

They drifted for a while and finally decided to shake things up by moving to Phoenix. It didn't work out. The marriage was already doomed. Megan's soon-to-be-ex was doing a lot of things he shouldn't have been doing. But Megan didn't want to tuck tail and run back to Ohio. It had taken her a lot of years to move back to Phoenix so she decided to stay.

She met Jordan on an online dating site during Bike Week three years ago and immediately, there was a connection. They loved spending time together. Jordan wasn't like anyone else Megan had met online. The following weekend was Easter. Since all of Megan's family was back east, she had planned to spend the weekend alone but Jordan insisted she come along to spend the day with his family. Three months into the relationship, Megan got pregnant.

She had been pregnant twice before when she was married and had miscarried both times. The first time, her ex put his arms around her, hugged her from behind and she felt the baby let go of its life. The second time she miscarried it felt differently, but Megan had been going on the assumption that she wasn't going to be able to carry a child. Jordan had a vasectomy many years before. He never anticipated becoming a father, either. Megan gave him the option to leave, expected him to question if the child was even his, but to his credit, Jordan stayed right by her side. And to their delight, their daughter, Avery, was born five weeks early, but otherwise completely healthy.

And that's when Megan picked up her final title: Avery's mom. She says it is the only title she's ever been okay with…but here's the deal: Although Megan feels as if she has always lived her life behind the titles of others, Megan is pretty amazing in her own right. She has large, soulful eyes and tattoos covering her arms. She's a therapist who helps others on their journey to becoming sober, just as she's been helped along the way. Being an alcoholic means she has an almost sixth sense about people. That guy who leans against the convenience store wall playing on his phone? Yeah, she knows he's a dealer. She sees him.

She is friend to the marred, the broken, and the obscure. When she goes to a different city and begins feeling lonely, she knows she can go to an AA meeting and immediately find acceptance. Megan likes haunted houses and drag queen bingo. It's not like she's a regular mom. She's hardworking and edgy with a ton of street smarts.

Life doesn't always turn out the way we expect but there's a beauty in that. When the unexpected is always just around the corner, it keeps us on our game. It never becomes boring. And as much as Megan feels like she hides in the shadows of others, she is living a life that shows others how interesting things can be if we take a few risks along the way.

The Girl That Has It All

Friend #37 – Jaye

When Jaye was a tween, her father had an opportunity to expand his business into the United States so he moved the family away from their beloved Canada to live in Arizona. There are a lot of things Jaye missed about her home country but mostly, she missed her friends.

Twenty years ago, there was no social media to keep up with people we once knew but Jaye found a way to communicate with those she knew in Canada through a series of chat rooms she found on the computer. It was all very innocent. Still, while she was exploring these chat rooms, she met a boy from Iowa online and they began chatting regularly. The two of them became very close over a period of time but after a while, they drifted apart as the young tend to do.

Then, when Jaye was sixteen, she got a message from this long, lost boy. He wanted to come out to Arizona to meet her. He had just turned eighteen, making him two years older than her. Jayc told her parents…and they panicked. Who wouldn't? Even Jaye, herself, said she would never let her own children meet a stranger from online. But eventually, her parents relented and the two were allowed to meet. Turns out, the boy wasn't a psycho. He was actually a pretty decent kid. They began dating long distance and eventually…they got married.

In a lot of ways, Jaye admits she is very lucky. She realizes she missed out on some things by finding her match so early on, but she's also had the opportunity for the two of them to grow up together. No one knows her better. Jaye is a CFO for a local non-profit. Her husband has his PhD. They own their own home and have two adorable children. They have a couple of Siamese cats. One of them may be schizophrenic. All in all, it's a pretty nice life...but lately, Jaye has been feeling sad for no particular reason. Her husband noticed it, too, leaving them both with a feeling that something was very wrong.

I applaud Jaye for having admitted this: She has actually been going to see a therapist. There is a stigma in our society that therapy is wrong but in reality, it is only the strong that have the courage to admit there are things out of their control that they don't understand. Out of therapy, Jaye realized her issues have been triggered by delayed grief. When Jaye was nineteen years old, her father died. The next day, Jaye packed her belongings and moved, giving herself no time to grieve.

And grief is an interesting thing. It is uncontrollable and often comes in like the waves of the ocean. Sometimes the waves recede into normalcy. Sometimes they are so overpowering one feels like they are going to drown. And it's okay to be sad. So often we fear sadness as if it is something that should never be...but it's normal. When someone you love dearly passes away, it's okay to feel depressed. It's okay to have days when you are overwhelmed with emotion. I don't know where the belief that we always have to be superwoman came from! We live in a world where sometimes unfortunate things happen. We do ourselves an injustice by not letting ourselves feel.

Jaye's learning some of this one day at a time. I get a sense that she can be quiet, a bookworm, maybe a tad analytical, and when you aren't the most outgoing person in the room, I would imagine it's harder to connect with people. Yet as Jaye sat across from me, I could feel my own humanity want to reach out and touch her, bring her comfort in some way.

This experiment of meeting one new person a week has taught me how important it is to have human connections in our lives. We all think we are so connected with social media but in reality, there are people like Jaye, who look like they have everything anyone could want…but still need someone to smile at them. They need to be distracted by the ridiculousness of other people's lives so they don't have to fall into the dark pit of their own emotions. They need a community that rallies around them, tells them they are cared for so they can feel the things they need to feel in order to fully heal.

I want a world like that.

The Single Mom
Friend #38 – Laurie

One of my long-time friends moved to a new neighborhood in Ahwatukee. Laurie and my friend, Angie, were introduced because they used the same realtor and live a few doors down from each other. Since the homes are new, the women have leaned on each other as they are exploring all the nooks and crannies of their new houses. Angie invited me to see a movie with her and at the last minute, asked Laurie if she would like to tag along. Angie knows I'm on a mission to meet new friends this year so she figured I wouldn't mind. And I didn't.

Originally from Chicago, Laurie grew up the youngest of three children. She graduated with a degree in math but trained in IT right out of college. Laurie had planned on moving in with a friend of hers and staying in Chicago, but her mother begged her to go to open interviews for a life insurance company based out of California that was doing interviews in the Chicago area. To appease her mother, Laurie went. They didn't have time for her that day but liked her resume enough to ask her if she was going to be in California anytime soon. As luck would have it, Laurie had a planned trip to California in two weeks so she scheduled an interview and she got the job! The salary they offered her was double what she was making in Chicago and the company was also offering to pay full moving expenses. Laurie was thrilled! And her parents were thrilled. Laurie didn't know it at the time but her mother was secretly plotting to move the entire family to the west coast. Which is exactly what eventually happened.

Laurie spent her twenties living and working in California. By her thirties, Laurie was ready to settle down. She met a man she thought she could love. They got married. Then they got pregnant. By that time, Laurie's mother had a new plot. She wanted the entire family to move out to Arizona, specifically Ahwatukee, Arizona. Laurie spent her pregnancy secretly flying to Arizona on the weekends to help with the house she and her husband were building. She wasn't planning to go back to work after her maternity leave. Her husband already had a job in Arizona. But just after their son, David, was born, her husband lost that job. In order to keep medical benefits and financial support for her newborn, Laurie was forced to keep her job in California. That meant flying out every Sunday night and flying back every Friday, leaving her newborn in Arizona.

Laurie's parents and her grandmother took care of David for the first nine months of his life. Laurie's husband wasn't much help. He often complained that the baby kept him awake. He wasn't very good at being a full-time dad. After nine long months, her husband finally found a job and Laurie was able to quit her job to become the full-time mother she had always wanted to be.

But things weren't so rosy on the home front. Laurie's husband was extremely resentful that he was the only bread-winner in the house. He complained it was too much pressure. As Laurie busied herself taking care of David, the couple grew apart and she suspected her husband of cheating long before she found the unassuming woman's voice on her answering machine telling her husband which hotel she was staying in. By that time, Laurie knew the marriage was over.

"Your girlfriend called," she told her husband, nonchalantly. "She left the address of the hotel she's staying in," she said, handing him the piece of paper.

Later that night, Laurie drove to the hotel and saw her husband's car sitting in the parking lot. Silently, in her car, she cried.

It was a nasty divorce. Her husband emptied out the bank accounts before she even considered it a possibility. For a while, she and David lived off credit cards in order to keep him in the only home he'd ever known. In the middle of the divorce, Laurie's soon-to-be ex-husband found out his father was dying so he rushed back to Oregon, but at the funeral, he informed Laurie he had decided not to return to Arizona. Laurie thought of that as a blessing until the judge in their divorce case ordered her to put her five-year-old on a plane alone once a month so he could see his father.

Laurie was also faced with having to find a new job after having been out of the work force for a few years…but that's when she caught a lucky break. The life insurance company she had worked for in California, called to see if she would consider returning to work. They were still based in California but in the 1990's there was this new thing called telecommuting and since Laurie was in IT, she could work from home in Arizona. In the beginning, the company did require her to fly in once a month in case there was an issue with month-end but eventually, even that came to a close. Laurie credits the money and stability of her job to be one of the things that got her through such a difficult time in her life. And she loves the analytics and the challenge of figuring out problems.

The other thing that got her through such a dark time in her life was her family. Every Saturday, they still meet for lunch at 12:30 to catch up on what has happened during the week. David is basically grown. He just graduated from college. One of the reasons Laurie bought a new house is because she is ready to begin her life as an empty nester. She has a light in her eyes and a buoyancy to her spirit. I could feel her excitement for this new phase brimming. It doesn't mean she loves her son any less. One of the reasons she wanted chat with me was because I've reinvented myself a few times job-wise. David now needs to find his first 'real' job and she wants to help him. She just doesn't know what advice to give him in this modern world because she's been with the same company for so long.

This house she just bought is the last house Laurie will ever buy. Now that she's raised David, the hard work is done. She no longer has to sacrifice and make the tough decisions because no one else will. Finally, she can be at peace on a job well done.

The Ray of Sunshine
Friend #39 – Patty

My hairdresser's salon is always a big party. There is a chaotic energy as soon as you walk through the door. Occasionally someone will bring in a little wine to share. And when it's your turn in the chair, the spotlight is on you. It's one of my favorite places.

One day back in the spring, my hairdresser began asking me about my project to meet fifty-two new friends. Patty wandered in about that time and when I was moved to the couch for my color to settle, I plopped down right beside her.

At the time, Patty was working for one of the local television stations. She has perfect blond hair and large, expressive eyes. I honestly can't remember what we talked about during that first meeting. It may have been her cats…but whatever it was, I instantly loved her. I was so excited when she agreed to be one of my new friends. We immediately connected on social media, but I could never get Patty to commit to a time to meet up so I could really get to know her.

I gathered through her social media page that she was the caretaker for both of her parents and that her father was extremely ill. And then the unthinkable happened. Patty's father passed away. That's the moment I stopped asking for Patty's time. I could tell through her posts that the sensitive soul I met for a moment, needed to take time for herself.

Months passed. And then, towards the end of summer, I was sitting in my hairdresser's chair, getting my hair blown out when Patty walked in the door. I immediately threw my hands in the air and shouted her name. She confessed that she had, indeed, been having a difficult time. "As soon as they let me out of this chair," I declared, "I'm going to come over there and give you a big hug!" Which is exactly what I did. And we arranged to meet up for drinks the following week.

Patty plopped down across from me declaring she was a hot mess. She didn't look like a hot mess. She looked newscaster professional, just as she always had. There wasn't a hair out of place but internally, I sensed there were choppy waters just below the surface.

Her older sister was in town which gave her some time apart from her mother, who she loves dearly. Her father had always been more of a struggle. In fact, during much of her life, Patty said they didn't really get along. She was always the black sheep of the family and she found her father to be…well…controlling. It says a lot about Patty's character that she was there for him, to bring him comfort in his last days. She says, in the end, her father's vulnerability made him more human, leaving all of the things that came before forgotten. There has to be some peace in that, to watch a relationship come full circle.

Patty was wearing a bright smile but I suspected grief had fractured her. She's an admitted introvert, a gentle soul. She is the type of person who would rather focus on the beautiful flower pushing its way through a concrete jungle world, which is ironic since her employer hunts out and reports on the most heinous of crimes against humanity.

One day a man approached Patty at work, asking about one of the on-air reporters. As those in television are trained to do,

Patty gave him no information. Stalking and harassment, unfortunately, aren't unusual for television personalities. But instead of focusing his anger elsewhere, the man turned his attention on Patty. He then began a series of actions that alarmed Patty and made her feel unsafe. It quickly came to her attention that the glass she sat in front of was not bullet proof and no amount of security measures that her employer suggested could put her at ease.

So she gave her notice at work. Having to live in fear is not what Patty wants to do with her life. All of this had happened in the short time between our last interaction. Its why Patty was feeling particularly out of sorts. And who wouldn't? All of her feelings are normal.

Then one day last week, Patty was driving home in the middle of one of Phoenix's monsoon storms and as the rain was crashing down onto her vehicle, she began to think about her dad. Suddenly, she noticed a butterfly, which you hardly ever see in Phoenix. It had its wing trapped under one of her wiper blades. As the blades frantically, moved back and forth to clear the rain from her windshield, the butterfly was being carried right along with them. So Patty pulled her little truck over in a convenience store parking lot and stepped out into the pouring rain, in her best suit, to free the butterfly's wing. As soon as it was free, it fluttered away and Patty stood there soaked, watching it, realizing it was a little like her life right now.

She's being bombarded with a lot of things that leave her feeling weak and soaked to the bone, yet she is still the kind-hearted, gentle soul that sees beauty in the world. In one word: She is lovely. Even with what she perceives to be a whirlwind of chaos encircling her, she knows it is only for a season. Patty said that the first half of a person's life is dedicated to doing what we think we are supposed to do. The second half of our lives is where we set boundaries so we can have the things we really want. She is just starting to set those boundaries and I can't wait to see the beautiful world she creates for herself on the other side of grief and chaos and transition.

The Chakradancer
Friend #40 – Emma

Emma was sitting outside waiting for me at the agreed-upon Starbucks when I arrived and as soon as she opened her mouth, her words dripped with a delightful English accent that she no longer realizes she has. Emma was born in the United Kingdom but her ex-husband's job was very specialized. They lived in Asia for a while until he was called back to the UK. Then, they were sent to Arizona…and at first, Emma wasn't sure she was going to like it here.

One of the first things she noticed was that Americans were particularly vocal and passionate about their politics. Of course, politics is a topic of conversation all over the world, but Emma was used to a level of civility in those that disagreed that she didn't find here in the United States. She likened it to rooting for a sports team. It was off-putting. Equally as oft-putting was the American take on religion. She was used to people keeping their religion relegated to their private moments but Americans tend to wear it as a badge of honor. When she was living in the city of Gilbert, people would often invite her family to church…but Emma didn't feel she really knew who these people were. She only knew them by their religion. Her beginnings in the United States really only worked to make her feel more disconnected.

Finally, Emma found a group that was different. It was led by a charismatic young man by the name of Alaric

Hutchinson, who Emma says has wisdom beyond his years. It is a judgment-free gathering where the foundation is peace, not love. I had to think about that one a bit. There's a lot of depth there. But it was in this place where Emma found peace in her life. Some people may believe she's a bit off her rocker, but she doesn't care what other people think. It's what she needed to do for herself. So she told Alaric she wanted to learn…and he taught her to be a master. Her expertise is in chakradance, which, as I understand it, is a holistic healing and well-being practice using movement, music and chakras. She admits her group has gotten smaller since Alaric moved to Colorado but every Sunday, the faithful meet to study and discuss how they can live a more peaceful life.

And Emma needed that foundation of peace because two years ago, her eighteen-year-marriage crumbled. It was a difficult time for her, particularly because she found, as I did, that some people treated her as if she had an infectious disease…as if divorce were contagious. With no family in the United States other than her two sons, Emma relied on her group for support and they rallied around her. Emma believes her desire to live a peace-filled life helped her get through the toughest parts of her divorce. But she admitted it wasn't a perfect transition. She is human, after all.

Her ex-husband was relocated to Australia and Emma considered moving there, too. Every sign pointed in that direction: The couple shares children together and it would make it easier to raise them if they were all on the same continent. Emma's mother was born in Australia so Emma would be able to get citizenship through descent. And let's face it, Emma's life in America hadn't really gone in the way a fairy tale goes. She was wondering if it was time to leave when one day, she wandered into a restaurant for breakfast. It was busy so in order to make things easier, she agreed to share a table with a man she didn't know. They inadvertently ordered the exact same breakfast …and they just clicked. It was instantaneous. Like they were meant to be together.

Emma never hides anything from her sons so after about six weeks, she invited the man to come to her house and meet them. He brought over enough food for an army and when he left, she broached the subject. She asked her sons how they would feel about her dating someone. Her eldest son knew immediately. He said he could tell by the way they looked at each other. Her younger son said he thought the man was nice because he had gone out of his way to bring them so much food.

And so Emma and her sons stayed in the United States. Her struggles are different now. She has become a school teacher assistant so she readily admits she isn't one that has a lot of money…but she has contentment. Even though the new man in her life is 33 years older than she is, he seems to be her match. And if you asked her, she would probably say all of the hardship she has faced while living in this country was part of the journey she needed to traverse in order to bring her to this place of well-being…because even the tallest mountain is still part of the journey.

The Crusader
Friend #41 – Jennifer

Jennifer barreled into the Chandler coffee shop full of purpose. After a quick stop to say hello to me at one of the tables, she was off on a mission to get herself a cup of coffee, leaving me trailing behind her to the cashier like an entranced child. After she had placed her order, she asked to speak to a manager. She's the PTO president for her child's school and they were scheduled to have a First Responder's Day on September 11th. She wanted to know if Starbucks would donate coffee to the event.

She's a tiny thing but she has a remarkable intensity. I immediately adored her.

Jennifer explained that her son goes to a local public school in the area. And it's a nice area! But it is in an older part of Chandler, Arizona, so the school is one of the older schools in the district. It was built in the 1970's and it is showing the wear and tear of age. In fact, the playground has been ripped out because it didn't meet current safety standards and because of budget cuts, it has never been replaced. Jennifer told me that even though the school is located in a relatively vibrant area of Chandler, the demographics of the children who go to this school are considered lower income. Why? Because the other families in Jennifer's neighborhood can afford to drive their children to newer schools. Actually, Jennifer could too…but that's not her style.

She works for a local nonprofit. She teaches a social injustice class at ASU. These days, with the current political climate, Jennifer claims the curriculum practically writes itself. So when no one wanted to step up as the PTO president, Jennifer did it. Not because she has so much time on her hands but because it was the right thing to do.

And she wants her kid to have a playground at his school. The Chandler School District had originally promised to replace the playground when it was taken out. Years later, the space still sits empty. All the newer schools in the district have playgrounds. Jennifer wonders if the children going to this school were from higher economic backgrounds if that playground would still be a dirt lot. The Chandler School District has now told them if they want a playground, the PTO is going to have to raise the thirty thousand dollars themselves, a task that seems almost insurmountable.

Yet given the passion in Jennifer's voice, I feel like she is going to find a way.

And I get the impression this isn't Jennifer's only cause. When her sister found herself married to a man with serious mental health issues, Jennifer packed her bags and traveled to Boston for a month to help her sister get through her divorce. When she learned of a woman going through a separation due to a domestic violence situation, she offered to help her out...even though this woman is a virtual stranger. She even has an old dog that her youngest son is allergic to that she can't bear to exile from the house because of the unfairness of uprooting the dog out of the only family and home she's ever known.

In my experience, people who care so much about others know what it's like to be treated unfairly...but Jennifer and I never talked about that. Every word she said was a reverberation of how she could help someone else, even though she has a marriage and two small children of her own. It was: 'What can I do? How can I help?' It was selfless.

And in almost exactly one hour, she looked at the time, said her goodbyes and rushed out the door to pick up more donations. I watched her leave with a bit of admiration stuck in the middle of my throat. I know in dark moments, Jennifer probably wonders if she is making a difference, not because of anything lacking on her part. Change happens slowly and I don't think it can keep up with the fiery trail Jennifer blazes.

Cast Out
Friend #42 – Leslie

I love it when my current friends refer me to people they think I may like. It gives me a chance to stalk those people a little on social media so I don't have to worry about lulls in the conversation. Leslie once worked with an old sorority sister of mine so after we set up an appropriate time and place to meet, I got online to check her out. The first thing that jumped out at me was that she works for a school I'd seen on the news recently. Once we'd both grabbed a drink from the bartender, I asked her what was going on.

Leslie is the digital coordinator for the school's online program. She told me that the school rented its building from the Phoenix school district and that the district had suddenly declared they were raising the school's rent by more than eight hundred percent. Leslie said, her boss, the principal, had been particularly stressed about it and was hoping to be able to reason with the school district during negotiations. The parents were stressed, thinking they might now have to find another school for their children. The children are stressed, thinking they may not be able to continue to attend school with their friends. But why would the Phoenix school district do that?

Leslie shrugged. The building is going to sit empty if her school moves out. Leslie suggested that maybe the school district is hoping to disperse their current student base into the Phoenix school district, enabling the district to get more funding. I had a different idea. Right now, downtown Phoenix is booming. New high-rise condo developments are popping up on every corner. Leslie admitted her school was in a prime location. I think a handshake deal has already been done between a developer and the district. Now all the Phoenix school district has to do is simply get Leslie's school out. I know it because I've seen deals like that in the past. It's how things in Arizona really get done.

Leslie and I shared a somber moment as we both let that sink in. Whatever is built in that place will have been built on the backs of children and their parents. And for what? It isn't likely that they will be building affordable housing.

But then again…life isn't always fair.

Leslie grew up in a good Mormon family, the youngest of four sisters. She admits she was always the little sister that questioned everything yet she still did the proper Mormon thing: She married and had children while she was young. Those early years were difficult but even then, Leslie believed in education. She helped put her husband through school and when he was finally established in his own career, Leslie began to voice her desire to get a higher education for herself. To her surprise, her husband disagreed. He didn't believe education was a good investment for women and finally told her, only because she was relentless, that if she wanted a higher education, she was going to have to pay for it herself. So she did. And the more knowledge she gained, the more she questioned things in her life…like her religion.

She finally told her husband that she didn't feel like she was still a believer and that she wanted to stop attending church. He told her that if they didn't believe in the same things, he didn't think they could remain married. So they divorced. That was eighteen years ago.

Leslie's children are grown now. She's actually in a pretty happy spot but the one thing she still struggles with is meeting new people. How do you meet new people unless you are online dating? The majority of Leslie's close friends are people she's met through work but she knows there are more people out there. She just doesn't know how to get to them.

Growing up in a religious group, she was surrounded by a loving and supportive community. It's an easy thing to take for granted until it's no longer there…and as soon as she left the religion, all those loving, supportive doors closed never to be re-opened again. The people she'd always thought would be there for her, weren't. There's a loneliness about that. The trust and ties of being part of a community is a very difficult thing to rebuild.

And now it seems her community is going to be broken up once again as her school will need to relocate. I know life changes and people change, but sometimes things are just so damn unfair! In the days after meeting her, I am still incensed at the unfairness. And I don't really have an answer except to say: be better, be kinder, be mindful of those around you. Two women can't solve the world's problems over cocktails but enjoyable, intelligent conversation does make us alive.

The Dancer & The Warrior
Friend #43 – Rayn

Rayn warned me she would be coming from a fitness class so she would be hot and sweaty. Wanting to make sure she was comfortable, I got up early and went to the gym before I headed over to meet her for coffee so I could be hot and sweaty too. Her Facebook page told the story of someone with fitness as a core part of their life and when she arrived, she told me she had considered an attempt to look her best, only to realize the sweaty girl with no makeup was more like her than anything else.

I admired that about her. I like people with transparency.

And so, to be perfectly transparent on my part, I admitted that I would only rate my fitness level at moderate at best. The little pillow of fat around my midsection was proof of it. Rayn shrugged, as if it didn't bother her. "I don't exercise to get smaller," she said. "I exercise to be more powerful." And by the way she moved her arms, I could virtually see the warrior inside of her step out in front of me and then fall back.

Rayn was trained as a professional dancer. She fell in love with modern dance at ASU and for a while, she even had her own dance company in the southwest. Then, nine years into her marriage, she unexpectedly got pregnant. Children had never been a part of the plan for her or her husband, but something about the timing felt right. They had both individually been feeling it. It could have been a deal breaker for her marriage but instead it brought them closer together. And for Rayn, that was very fortunate because it was emotionally difficult for her, a person who had always been so expressive with her body, to have that body and her hormones change in unexpected ways.

She was lying in bed after her first pregnancy when she told her husband, "If we want another child, we need to have them right away…because otherwise, I don't think I can do this again." Rayne had a second little girl soon afterwards but the hardship of both pregnancies left her derailed mentally.

Rayn admits there is probably something chemically wrong with her brain. She can feel the depression coming on like the flu. Sometimes she denies the symptoms but more recently, she recognizes them and tries to hold them at bay. Depression still has a way of poking its pesky way through. Sometimes she has had to resort to medication to ride out the wave…and she feels no shame in admitting that. For her, a balanced diet and exercise help her keep her emotions in check.

Rayn teaches fitness classes in the Chandler area and when she is in front of her class, she is at her best and most positive. She said some of the women in her classes would probably be shocked to know that there are times after class when she cries and has a difficult time at home. It doesn't hold her back. It's just something she knows she has to manage. And aren't we all managing something?

Every day is a balancing act to manage children, relationships and ambition. Give too much to one area and another area suffers. Right now, Rayn is traveling around from studio to studio to teach her classes, toting all of her gear around in her van. She would like nothing more than to have her own studio. Some of the women in her classes have pointed out there is a fancy new shopping plaza not far away that would be perfect for a fitness studio. But Rayn likes the women she meets working out of the rec center. She feels like it is where she makes the most difference.

Once, before Rayn met her husband, she was engaged to another man who one day, out of the blue, dumped her and quickly removed everything from the apartment they shared together. Rayn remembers sitting cross-legged on her bare mattress, because he had taken the sheets, with tears rolling down her face. There were no dishes in the cabinets. Her family was far away. She felt like it was rock bottom, like she had nothing. It was a pivotal moment. Yet the women in her dance troop scooped her up, and piece by piece, put her back together.

Now at 45, Rayn's body doesn't do all the things it used to be able to do but her greatest performance is the one she never realized she was giving. There have been moments in her life that have been ugly, hurtful and filled with tears...but there have also been moments when her heart has been filled with love for her husband and her children. There have been moments of depression and moments when she's walked away from a class, feeling as if her instruction has helped someone else. It is the dance we all perform called life. It's the dance that is the most important, the yin and the yang, but it is the balance that makes it most beautiful.

The Ignited
Friend #44 – Jennifer

Five years ago, Jennifer was a music teacher in Indiana who wanted to change her school, but because there was no shortage of music teachers in Indiana, that was a very difficult thing to do. She had just started dating a guy she really liked when she found out he was being forced to relocate to Arizona for a job. Spurred on at the notion of losing the guy, Jennifer looked for a job as a music teacher in Arizona and to her surprise, she found one. The couple continued to date after they both moved to Arizona. Eventually, they moved in together and got engaged. And if the story had ended there, I could have said that was the most daring thing Jennifer had ever done, that she had a nice, quiet life.

But these are the times when being a teacher in Arizona has become synonymous with being a revolutionary. Jennifer has seen firsthand how programs have been cut and how students' education has suffered at the lack of funding in our Arizona schools. What started out as murmurs in the hallways has led to red shirts and negations. Jennifer was never a leader of the movement but she was moved by the spirit of it. It was a cause she quietly, deeply believed in.

And then in April, negotiations broke down among teachers and legislators. Reluctantly, the teachers began calling for a walkout. Jennifer heard the mutterings of her fellow teachers. They were nervous. How would their students feel about them abandoning their classrooms? How would their families live without the support of their meager paychecks? Jennifer had no children. She had a fiancé she split half of the bills with so she felt if anyone could afford to be made a sacrifice, it was her. She was ready to lose her job for what she believed in.

Of course, she had to talk to her fiancé before making any major decisions. He nodded sympathetically as she pleaded her case and then told her if she lost her job, he would only give her thirty days to find another one. Thirty days?!?! Jennifer couldn't promise that. She had no idea how long the walkout would go on and if she was committed, she was committed to the end. That entire conversation changed the way Jennifer saw her fiancé. She didn't want to be married to a man who couldn't see the vision in what she was trying to do. She didn't want to be with someone who was unsupportive when the chips were down. Jennifer and her fiancé broke up soon afterwards. It didn't stop her from walking out when she was called on rather it fueled her footsteps all the way down to the Arizona capital.

Jennifer didn't lose her job in the walkout but it did ignite a fire within her that she didn't realize she had. Her social media page is a monument to the campaigning warrior she has become yet when she sat across from me in the restaurant, she still looks like a shy, Midwestern girl. There is nothing that says extraordinary about her except the fire in her eyes and the passion in her voice.

She feels like being a teacher these days makes her part of a sisterhood, a community. Not long ago, Jennifer was at a gas station and noticed that a woman had a #RedforEd bumper sticker on the back of her vehicle. Jennifer asked her about it and before either of them knew it, they were locked in conversation about the Red for Ed movement. The woman was a teacher from another school. Jennifer asked her about the issues she and fellow teachers were facing. It was only a brief conversation but a few months ago, these women would have passed each other like ghosts. Now they have a foundation of commonality.

Jennifer is supporting three pro-education candidates who are running for office. They are: Kelli Butler, Christine Marsh and Aaron Lieberman. In order to get them elected, she has undertaken the challenge of physically knocking on people's doors and talking to them about the issues. She told me they go out in pairs with an ap on their phones telling them a little bit about who is in each house. One of the doors Jennifer had knocked on that day had a man living there who was a Democrat and a woman living there who was a Republican.

Nervously waiting on the front step, Jennifer prayed the man, who was a Democrat, would answer the door. She thought the man would be easier to sway but it was the woman who peered out at them.

Jennifer tried engaging her in conversation but the woman interrupted, "What are these candidate's stance on education?" she asked.

Jennifer said, "They are all pro-education. I'm actually a teacher myself."

The Republican woman smiled and opened her door wider. "My children are teachers and I've about had it with how they've been treated."

Jennifer smiled reliving the story because she had faced her fear and made a difference.

After the election, Jennifer isn't sure what she's going to do next. She has some ideas…but tomorrow is more important. She feels like, at 36, she's finally come out of her shell and now that she's been ignited, there's no turning back.

The Solider
Friend #45 – Sean

Sean was one of fourteen children born to his parents. It was a crowded, chaotic household, but it was still filled with a lot of love. When he was a kid, he used to collect bottles from his neighbors so he might be able to turn them in for enough money to buy candy. It was a rather ingenious scheme until his mother got wind of it. She grounded him saying that begging for bottles made the family look poor. But they *were* poor. There were a lot of mouths in the house to feed. All of Sean's clothes were hand-me-downs and he was grateful for the half of one drawer he was given to store his things in the bedroom he shared with his brothers.

After the stint with bottle collecting, Sean's mother decided he was old enough to follow in the footsteps of his older brothers and allowed him to take on a paper route. Sean used it, as his brothers had before him, to build relationships with the homeowners and to stake out a market he could milk for a lawn mowing business. If competition ever moved into his territory, his older brothers, who were bigger than him, helped to intimidate the competition right out. And Sean loved working! It gave him the opportunity to buy things for himself like store-bought new clothes and a baseball glove, things that he'd never had before. Sean had always wanted to play sports when he was in school but there was too much work and never enough money in the household for him to do it.

After high school, he enrolled in the army. It was the only way he knew how to give himself a college education. He actually spent his eighteenth birthday in Korea and by this twentieth birthday, he'd quickly risen through the army ranks. He was smart…and he showed promise, but his time in Vietnam blemished his soul. I guess it would scar anyone. It was during this time in his life he picked up smoking because why not smoke when any moment could be your last? And there were a lot of moments when he feared for his life, saw things decent human beings weren't meant to see. It was a moment by moment reel of reality so horrifying that he became resentful of the people who sent him there. He wasn't even sure the war he was fighting was for a just cause. It was a war he protested when he came back…but he never forgot his brothers on the front lines. In fact, he said any time he runs into a person who has given service to this country, he feels a kinship with them, a bond to protect them and theirs.

He eventually returned home from the war and he met a woman whose childhood was very different from his own. She came from a wealthy family. She was college educated. Sean said he believed she was smarter than he was. Perhaps, that's where he went wrong. But he loved her. The couple married and had four children together, each exactly four years apart. He loved his children and really wanted to be a good father. He took parenting classes when they were young and made sure his children had the opportunity to play sports while they were in school, an opportunity he never had.

He was married to his wife for over twenty years. Then one day he woke up and realized no one liked her. She had grown increasingly condescending over the years and Sean was tired of always being in the middle. They divorced and his wife married someone new exactly one month later. It was just too much for Sean. Everything in that area reminded him of the life he no longer had so he moved out to Phoenix to start again. He got a job in medical sales. He earned a master's degree. He was financially successful enough that he retired early. Essentially, he recreated his life.

Sean's backyard is a garden of angel statues. It brings him peace and comfort to sit among them. In fact, they are so important he brought along a marble statue of an angel with him. He pointed out the intricate grooves and details. An artist somewhere once had to look at a slab of marble and see the angel within it. That artist then had to carefully peel away the layers in order to create the masterpiece that sat before me. Our lives are like that. We are born blank slates and piece by piece we create our lives as we want them to be.

Sean didn't begin his life with a lot of advantages. He credits the things he has achieved to hard work and education. I imagine he wakes up every day determined to be a better person than he was the day before. Of course, that doesn't mean his life is without trial and tribulations but he often thinks back to his time in the military. He thinks, "If I can make it through Vietnam and live through it, then surely I can make it through anything." Nothing scares him now. He's still a soldier. The difference is he's now a soldier of his own making.

The One That Matters
Friend #46 – Gigi

Gigi wanted to meet up and do something fun so I suggested Rustler's Rooste, a cowboy-themed restaurant with amazing views. She'd lived in Phoenix her entire life and had never been there. Looking around as the cotton candy and balloon animals were passed from table to table, Gigi proclaimed the restaurant wasn't a place where a little Mexican girl would normally go. Gigi's father is Caucasian and her mother is Mexican…but she wasn't the only person of color in the restaurant that night. I thought the statement was odd.

Gigi was recommended to me through another friend. Physically, she is a solid woman but even dressed down in a t-shirt and jeans, I could see she had a loveliness buried under a hard exterior. Of course, none of that was my first impression. The first thing I noticed was that when she sat across from me, even though the table was very small, she seemed very far away.

I babble when I'm nervous, and in an effort to make Gigi feel more comfortable, my chatterbox wound itself up. I wasn't exactly sure how to do it but I wanted to see what was on the other side of Gigi's wall. Slowly, she began open up and as she told me about her life, venom seeped around the edges of her stories. I don't think it was intentional. It was poison that had been held back for a very long time. I don't think she even knew it was there.

"People don't like what I have to say," Gigi blurted out. But I did. I like blunt people. You don't have to wonder if there is a façade they are hiding behind.

Gigi is a school teacher and once, not long ago, a male teacher was teaching his students how to build a playhouse. Gigi could tell it wasn't going to work so she told him the way he was doing it was wrong. The man was so offended that she'd questioned him, he took the disagreement to the principal. He yelled and screamed while she sat angrily silent, and in the end, she was the one who was asked to move to another classroom.

I could tell by the way she told the story she was angry no one had taken her side.

When Gigi was in college, she had gotten a scholarship for track and field. I wasn't surprised. She exudes strength but she admitted she has a tendency to giggle, particularly when she is nervous. She was tossing the medicine ball back and forth with another girl at the gym. The coach had already yelled at her, thinking her giggling meant she wasn't taking her training seriously, but the scolding only increased Gigi's involuntary laughter. Finally, the coach threw a medicine ball at the back of Gigi's head in frustration. The impact caused a tearing of her tendons and muscles, a particularly painful injury…yet there was no apology, no retribution. It was if her pain and suffering didn't matter.

A math degree was the quickest way out of her scholarship and away from that coach, so that's the path Gigi chose.

When Gigi was a child, she asked her father what the most valuable thing in his life was. He thought about it for a while, narrowing it down to four items. After debating back and forth for a minute, he told Gigi he couldn't possibly choose between his house and his car because they were both valuable in their own ways. Innocently, Gigi looked at him and asked, "Why didn't you say your family?" The verbal lashing she received afterwards was second to none. Gigi learned right then never to ask sincere questions again. Or at least not to ask questions when she already knew the answer. Yet she never heard him apologize. It's no wonder Gigi has spent a lifetime believing she doesn't matter.

But the cherry on top of all of the wrongs done to Gigi was when she was a child, she was molested by a priest. Gigi held in that secret for a long, long time. It ate away at her. It changed her as a person. And when she finally worked up enough courage to tell her mother, her mother said, "That's too bad." TOO BAD??? Out of all different types of unfairness, that one deserves the most outrage! But that isn't the reaction Gigi got. In a climate where a potential Supreme Court justice is accused of sexual assault and then still gets to sit on the highest court in the land, there's a lot of people who begin to feel as if they don't matter. And the hate that is spewed is a natural reaction from victims never heard. And there are a lot of victims.

And that brick wall Gigi has up? The one I felt immediately when she sat down? It's there for a reason. There's been so much unfairness in her life that if I were in her shoes, I'd be distrustful of people too. I didn't pity her because she doesn't call for any. She's a tough chick. She teaches in one of the toughest school districts in all of Phoenix where she receives some of the highest teaching scores in the entire state. She's smart…and if people were more sensible, they would be listening to her. And the anger? I'm no therapist but sometimes, I think people just need to get all of that crap out of them so they can live a lighter, more productive life.

In Gigi's classroom, sixty percent of the kids are Hispanic and forty percent of them are white. One day, Gigi could tell the Hispanic side of the classroom wasn't paying attention so she said to them, "Listen, you are bilingual. If I can just get you through school, you will make more money than your white counterparts." One of the little boys on the white side of the room then blurted out, "Yeah…at McDonald's." The class started laughing. Gigi turned to the Hispanic side of the room and she saw the looks on their faces. They believed the white kid.

Gigi matters. Those kids matter. People matter. Instead of being so quick to judge, maybe we should just listen…because we never know what other people have been through. And that night, saying goodbye to Gigi in the parking lot, I really just wanted to hug her tight and tell her there are good people out there in the world. But I can't promise that. Gigi has to find them on her own. But maybe I can change a little of her perception by just showing her the good in me.

The Good Girl
Friend #47 – Emily

Emily is a good girl. She grew up in a Christian home in San Diego and met her husband while he was stationed there. He's a small-town boy from Missouri. She admits he doesn't talk very much, as country boys tend to be on the quieter side, but the pair shares the same values. They love Jesus and more than anything Emily wants to create a home that is comfortable for them, their families and their friends.

They married when Emily was twenty-three and they tried living in Missouri for a while. Being from San Diego, Emily wasn't a fan of the humidity and cold winters. Her husband isn't a fan of big cities, but Queen Creek, Arizona seems to be the best of both worlds. The desert climate is nice most of the year and although Queen Creek does have a lot of the city's amenities, it is still far enough outside of Phoenix to have ample farmland and horse property that make Emily's husband feel right at home.

For the most part, Emily has a happy life. She mostly has the life she grew up believing she would. She has a loving husband and a job she finds meaningful. The only thing missing from Emily's life is…a baby.

At one point she went to the doctor, complaining something was wrong. She had gained one hundred pounds in a year. The doctor dismissed her, sent her home and told her to eat less. Still, Emily persisted. Eventually, she was diagnosed with polycystic ovarian syndrome which is basic terminology for your hormones go crazy…but it also makes a woman less likely to conceive. Over the years, Emily has been poked with needles, scheduled for endless tests and filled her gullet with an obscene number of pills. Nothing worked. At one point, she did become pregnant only to lose the baby before it was born. I sat across from her, stunned, my heart aching but Emily was surprisingly nonchalant about it.

"I'm over it," she said.

I guess there are only so many tears a person can cry.

These days, Emily has lost her belief in Western medicine. Acupuncture is what has helped her the most. She's also recently cut dairy and gluten from her diet. Her skin has cleared up. She's beginning to lose some of the weight. She even feels stronger. She admits she still isn't at the weight she wants to be, but then again, when she was a size four, she wasn't at the weight she wanted to be either. Yet she's a beautiful girl with bright eyes and big dimples. I think Emily would be beautiful no matter what size she was.

She'll be turning thirty soon. When she was young, she thought she'd have four children by now but most days, she's pretty content curling up with her three dogs. I think she'd still like a baby if she was blessed with it, but I also think she's grown past the emotional frustration of attempting to force something that may not be meant to be. Instead, she focuses her time on helping others because deep down in her heart, I believe Emily knows that everyone has the choice of whether to be happy or whether to be miserable. Emily chooses happiness. And the rest she leaves up to God.

The Model
Friend #48 – Taryn

Taryn was a sickly child. Early on, the doctors realized she was allergic to eggs, peanuts and corn. Think about that. Almost everything Americans eat contains some form of eggs, peanuts and corn. And it wasn't just a small allergy. As a child, Taryn remembers ingesting any form of corn would literally make her skin burn. It was like her body rejected the one thing that would nourish her: food.

Luckily, her mom loves to cook. Twenty years ago, there were few options for those with food allergies but Taryn's mom found clever substitutions. And slowly, the skinny kid became stronger. The food allergies didn't go away but Taryn learned how to manage them. By the time she was in junior high, Taryn didn't feel like the sickly kid she used to be…and she wasn't.

Taryn's older sister had always been in dance so when the older sister expressed interest in belly dancing, Taryn's mom decided Taryn would also benefit from the instruction…and Taryn loved it! Nowadays, we think of the Middle Eastern culture as ultraconservative but it is also the culture that gave us belly dancing and Arabian Nights. Taryn learned the artistry of the dance. She was captivated by its movement, its beauty. She learned how the dance differed from country to country, how the Egyptian dance is very different from the Lebanese dance. And Taryn became quite skilled at it.

When she was seventeen, she was belly dancing on a stage when she collapsed and went into anaphylactic shock. Luckily, her mother was sitting in the audience and was well-prepared for such an emergency. I suppose she would have to be with a child so sensitive to certain foods. Still, the collapse was unnerving, particularly because Taryn knew she had not ingested any eggs, peanuts or corn before the performance. The doctors were baffled. Taryn took it easy for a while but eventually wanted to get back to dancing. Once again, she was triggered into anaphylactic shock. It happened a few times, actually, and always when she was exerting herself. The doctors began to dig deeper. Taryn's mother asked lots of questions. Finally, Taryn went to Southwest College of Naturopathic Medicine where she was tested again for food allergies and the results not only confirmed her reaction to eggs, peanuts and corn, but they also noted there were other foods that give a delayed shock to Taryn's system, particularly when she exerts herself.

So Taryn's diet became even more restrictive. Because of the food allergies she has lived with her entire life, Taryn is lean. And tall. Well, she's taller than me which doesn't necessarily make her super tall…but her lanky body gave rise to another profession. One of the women she met through belly dancing had a husband who was a photographer. One day, one of the husband's models bailed on him at the last minute so his wife suggested he call Taryn in as a replacement. She stepped in and really enjoyed the modeling experience. That one gig created the opportunity for another and pretty soon, Taryn had a career as a model.

After moving out of her mother's house, Taryn found a roommate named Wendy. Wendy always lit up the room but she also hated being alone. In fact, Wendy was almost always seen with an entourage surrounding her. She loved being around people and Taryn couldn't imagine anyone happier. Then, one day, Taryn went to L.A. for a job and when she returned, she was intercepted by some friends before she could get to her front door. While Taryn had been away, Wendy had killed herself in their apartment. The demons in Wendy's head had finally gotten to her. She had always used people as the buffer to her own thoughts but with no one around, Wendy lost the fight…and her death deeply affected Taryn.

Maybe it affected her because they had been so close, yet Taryn hadn't realized the mental torment her roommate was going through. Maybe it affected Taryn because it hit so close to home. One peanut without the right medical treatment and Taryn might have had a similar fate.

When I think of models, I think of the shell of a person, someone who has learned to convey beauty on the outside. But Taryn is so much more than that. She is sweet, down to earth and deeply soulful. When Wendy died, modeling became more about artistry and making the onlooker of the photograph feel something inside of themselves rather than just a picture. Taryn has gone on to model in personally meaningful shoots for breast cancer awareness and suicide prevention. Her photographs typically reveal a message. It is an art unlike anything I've known but seems in keeping with Taryn's love of movement and expression. When you look at Taryn's photos, she wants the onlooker to see there is more to her than just a pretty face…because she IS more than just a pretty face. She is the emotional tide running deep in us all.

The Reluctant Dad
Friend #49 – Dan

It was pouring rain on the day I was supposed to meet Dan. The small coffee shop I'd picked out was crammed with people trying to avoid what was falling from the sky. Somehow, I managed to claim a small table in the middle of the noisy chaos. I was just beginning to think the timing of this meeting was bad when Dan lowered his black umbrella and walked in.

If you saw Dan in a crowd of people, you would probably overlook him, but he has a way about him that took me back to my Midwestern roots, to a time when I only knew people were good, solid and dependable. He seemed to be half man, half twelve-year-old boy, although I'd estimate his age to be relatively close to mine. He'd been sent to me through another friend of mine who told me Dan had triplets. That's really the only thing I knew about him. He is conspicuously absent on social media.

I gave him a minute to settle in and he ordered a cup of coffee, which is apparently a rarity for him. Dan never really wanted children, but now that he has three seven-year-old girls, he can't imagine his life without them.

It all started back when his sister announced she was pregnant. Dan's longtime girlfriend had always wanted nothing more than to be a mother so watching Dan's sister go through the joy of her pregnancy brought feelings to the surface that had long been suppressed. Dan's girlfriend had been married once before and had gone through two miscarriages. The pair always knew if they were ever going to have children, it was going to be an uphill battle.

They had been together for over a decade. Dan's girlfriend had always been upfront about wanting to be a mother. It was never something she hid and now with his girlfriend in such a shambles over his sister's pregnancy, Dan began to feel guilty about wasting so much of her time. Ten years is an awfully long time to wait. So, Dan agreed to fertility treatments thinking one child wouldn't be so bad. Three babies were never in the plan. In fact, Dan was very specific on NOT planting too many embryos in an effort to prevent multiples. When the doctor informed them that they were expecting triplets, Dan immediately looked towards the heavens for answers. What had they done?

Dan's girlfriend was forty-two years old. They didn't even know if her body could carry three babies and as the days turned into weeks, his girlfriend's body began changing and expanding at an alarming rate. In the last days of her pregnancy, she couldn't even walk. And there was nothing Dan could do but watch in horror as the pregnancy unfolded.

The babies came at 31 weeks. Fertility babies almost never go full term. Each baby girl was born at two to three pounds apiece. They were the most fragile things Dan had ever seen. Up until that point, he had never held a regular newborn baby, much less a preemie. He was afraid to touch them but one particularly brusque neonatal nurse saw him hovering on the sidelines at feeding time, "Come on, dad," she said. "I'm busy. You're going to have to help feed them." In the moment, Dan didn't know how to say no...and that's the first time he ever fed one of his daughters. It would not be the last.

The babies came home at 40 weeks. One baby is overwhelming. Three babies are all-consuming. Suddenly, the world began to revolve around feedings and diaper changes. As soon as one baby was sleeping soundly, another would start to cry. Dan hired an overnight nurse to come in two nights a week. He said he thinks it was the only time he and his girlfriend ever slept. And the overnight nanny was non-stop busy.

By the time, Dan's girls were three-years-old the strain of parenthood had taken its toll on Dan's relationship. His girlfriend took their girls and moved out. Those early days of the split were full of animosity. His girlfriend wanted full custody of the children. Dan had to fight bitterly for his rights as a father, but at the end of the day, a fair agreement was finally reached. Now that his daughters are seven-years-old, he realizes that even though he and the mother of his children have their differences, their parenting styles are strikingly similar. They get along much better being apart.

He doesn't date, preferring to shower all of his attention on his daughters. They are his world. And they seem to be good kids. Dan's mother lives next door to him and he's developed a strong community through his church, giving him a solid, happy life with only a mild amount of chaos. Being a single dad of triplets wasn't the plan, but he fell in love with those three little ponytailed girls who have given his life sparkle and meaning. I know three girls is a lot of work...but what a wonderful blessing! Now that he is on the other side of it, Dan has realized how fulfilling being a parent can be. I guess the road to parenthood is different for everyone. Some people just have a different way of getting there.

The Son
Friend #50 – Derek

I was picking up tacos for a business meeting. The restaurant didn't have them ready so I stood talking with the guy working behind the window. He was a nice-looking young man with an easy way about him. I gathered he was the restaurant owner's son. While we were chatting, I mentioned my mission to meet 52 new friends this year. His eyes widened and sparkled. "I want to be number fifty," he declared.

So, we agreed to meet up for coffee. But in order to understand the son, I quickly learned I would first have to know about the father.

Derek's father grew up in a small, poverty-stricken town in a Mexico. By the age of 6, he was already leading a herd of sheep across the Mexican terrain on a daily basis and working as a sheep herder. His father loved soccer as boy, but there was never any money to buy him soccer shoes. By Derek's account, his grandfather was an alcoholic. It was a bad situation for Derek's father so at the age of fourteen, he illegally crossed the border into the United States with a group of twenty-year-old young men. They were all looking for a better life.

Derek's father found work in a restaurant in San Diego. He was a smart kid. He was a hard worker and he saved his money. In 1988, he bought a failing Mexican franchise restaurant. It was in a rough neighborhood, peppered by gang violence, Bloods and Crypts, but Derek's father stood up to them in a way that earned the gang's respect. Instead of folding, the restaurant flourished and in 1991, Derek's father dumped the franchise name and changed the signage to reflect his family name.

Derek's father went back to Mexico as a success, wanting to be an example to his people but his own father condemned him saying no one could earn that type of money unless they sold drugs. Derek's father was deeply hurt. He'd become successful despite the odds and his own family had turned against him.

But instead of dwelling in defeat, Derek's father carried on. He moved the family to Arizona to open more restaurants. In fact, Derek grew up in the restaurant. At first, he observed by sitting on crates in the backroom. As he got older, he learned how to take orders. Then, he learned how to cook. Then, his father took him under his wing and taught him how to manage…but some lessons are best learned on your own.

Derek went to ASU and graduated with an accounting degree becoming the first member of his family to do so. He got a job working for an accounting firm, which was exciting at first, but as time went on, Derek realized his company wasn't really paying him what he was worth. He became disenchanted with corporate America. His father always told him if you put a lot into your business, you will get a lot out of that business…but no one at the accounting firm was putting much into Derek.

Derek knew his father owned rental houses so if any of his employees found themselves in a spot without a roof over their heads, his father would step in and give them a place to stay. If an employee was having a hard time getting to work, Derek's father would buy them a car and let them make payments. His father's philosophy rewarded hard work, gave those employees a chance at a better life and inspired their loyalty. Derek's father is beloved by his employees because he cares about them.

So, when Derek was called in for a performance review at the accounting firm, there was a mutual parting of ways. Now, at 28, Derek owns his own marketing company that has given his father's restaurants a boost in customers by revolutionizing them with modern marketing concepts. There are now five restaurants in total, and Derek and his father have plans to open more. I don't want to give off the impression that this has been an easy road for Derek's family. There have definitely been big highs and devastating lows. But Derek's dreams are so much larger than his father's dreams ever were. He envisions a future growing the restaurant. He wants to expand his marketing business and open his own accounting firm. He's smart and understands people, probably very much like his father.

And as Derek was talking, all I could think about was how the current political climate claims only criminals come illegally through our Southern border. When I think of Derek's father and Derek, as an extension, I see only a family committed to working hard, providing good jobs and being kind to those who need a helping hand. Isn't that the type of people we WANT in this country? Isn't that the American dream?

And as we sat there, Derek casually mentioned how much tougher it is to illegally cross the border now. When his father crossed many years ago, the average price of passage over was $200. Now the average price of passage is between $8,000 and $20,000. The cartels are the only ones able to get anyone through. As I sat there, a thought entered my little white-bred mind. The reason we are seeing so much criminal activity surrounding illegal immigration is because the criminals are the only ones who can afford the price to get through. By being so restrictive, we have essentially blocked out the good.

I felt my jaw go slack. I'd never thought about it before.

Mostly, I think it's about being afraid of the unknown. We see the differences in culture and skin color, and we become afraid of each other without uttering a word. We listen to the media sources instead of just talking to one another, learning about each other, understanding one another. Meeting so many people from different walks of life has taught me to be less judgmental and sometimes, like on this day, people teach me things I never otherwise would have learned. Making a point to talk to strangers has changed my life...but I think Derek already knows how to do that. It's actually pretty incredible what a twenty-eight-year-old can teach you if you just take the time to listen.

The Organic Friend
Friend #51 – Keira

Keira is a business contact. We had our first phone call more than a year ago. She had just started her job working in the marketing department of an event center and I was the contact on file. There was something about the melody of her voice that made me immediately like her. In fact, I think I may have even suggested grabbing a drink at one point early on…but it was said in passing. I don't think she took me seriously.

We didn't meet face-to-face until April or May of this year, and it was specifically for business as we sat across from one another in her conference room. We went through the business at hand and when we were almost done, Keira made mention of the fact that she was single. That caught my attention. She is a beautiful redhead. We are close to the same age and neither of us have any children.

I'd been wanting to find someone to go with me to social events for singles and Keira was perfect! We scheduled in some time to meet up for cocktails in a Sex-in-the-City type restaurant in downtown Chandler.

Surprisingly, Keira has had worse luck with men than I have. She was engaged nine years ago but it didn't work out. She's been single ever since. Some of it was due to her former job. Keira was a roadie for several big bands including The Eagles, which meant she was constantly traveling all over the world. She enjoyed the work but it made it difficult to meet anyone special. She had taken the job at the local event center so that she could settle down and find true love…but that wasn't working out so well. Like me, she had tried nearly every online dating site out there. She'd been on dozens, if not hundreds, of dates. No one was the right fit and after a while, it was just frustrating. A person starts to imagine there is something wrong with them. And then they get impatient with the people they meet because it is so frustrating to constantly be on the single girl hamster wheel.

I knew all this because I was in the exact same situation.

Over drinks that night, Keira and I began to think about dating outside of the box. What are things we could do to meet single men organically? We came up with some ideas and scoped out a couple of singles groups. We even went to a pool party for singles at some random person's house. At that party, I was sitting next to Keira as she was talking to a very handsome, age appropriate man. The conversation was going really well until she asked him about his work travel schedule.

"To be honest," the man said. "I'm sick of traveling. Mostly, I just want to stay at home." In my head, I could hear the bullet crackle as he shot himself in the foot. I knew Keira was specifically looking for someone who enjoyed traveling.

Then, we both got busy with work, with life, with meeting new people. I sort of lost touch with Keira for a while when, out of the blue, I got a message from her asking me if I'd like to go with her to a speaking engagement. Of course, I agreed, and during the back-and-forth conversation, Keira casually mentioned she had been seeing someone that wasn't able to attend. I was intrigued so we agreed to meet up for dinner before the event.

Keira told me in the time we had been out of touch she'd let the crushing disappointment of online dating get to her. She'd even shut down all of her accounts but one that she wasn't checking regularly. She had finally settled into the notion that she would be a lonely cat lady for the rest of her life when she got a message from Sam asking her to coffee. It was abrupt, but Keira had been doing the online dating thing so long she was tired of wasting her time building someone into the person she wanted them to be, only to realize they weren't anything like the expectation she had for them when she met them in person. So, Keira said yes. And as always, she was hopeful but the repetition and history of her dating life gave her trepidation. She walked into the coffee shop expecting to be disappointed…but this time it was different.

Sam had been divorced for two years. He has two children, one in college and one who is a senior in high school. He's Swedish and loves to travel. In fact, they have so much in common that halfway through their coffee, Keira stopped him and said she'd like to see him again. And after five weeks of dating, Keira has now found herself in a committed relationship, something she hasn't had for a very long time.

I never set out to make Keira one of my 52 new friends. Our friendship evolved so naturally I didn't even think about it, but that evening as we hugged goodbye and parted ways in the dark parking lot, I watched Keira walk away from me. The breeze played with her long red hair. There was bounce in her step. She was headed home to pack a suitcase. Sam was flying her to New York to take her to see Hamilton on Broadway. I watched as Keira walked right into her own fairytale, my heart bursting with happiness for her, as only a friend's heart could.

UPDATE: As you, the reader, might be aware, this is real life, not a fairytale. Eight weeks into this new relationship, Keira and Sam broke up when she realized Sam had been seeing someone else. Dating over the age of forty is hard. I could see the pain in Keira's eyes. I could feel it. I've been there. I desperately want her to find someone she can love, someone who is more careful with her heart and I know when the timing is right, she will. It just isn't today.

The End
Friend #52 – Chris

I was walking back from lunch with a friend sometime in the spring of this year. My friend was talking about being in love. "When was the last time you were in love?" they asked.

I paused, thinking, trying to be honest with myself. "I don't know. Maybe fifteen years ago? But that may have been more obligation than love. I'm not sure I've ever really been in love."

My friend stopped walking and stared at me, mouth gaping open. "I feel sorry for you."

There's been a lot of times in my life that I've wondered if something is wrong with me. I think I can be charming. I think I can be well-liked. But when it comes down to having a deep, personal relationship with anyone, I have been an absolute failure. Mostly, I feel like the major relationships that have come into my life have cared about me for surface reasons and nothing more. It has left me empty.

But the optimist in me never lets me give up. It is the reason I continued to stay on the online dating hamster wheel. And let's be honest, I met a lot of good guys. They just weren't the right connection for me…which was frustrating. I wanted someone to fit but I no longer needed someone to fit. And after a while, dating is more tedious than it is fun.

I was sitting down with Friend #20 when I made a negative comment about my dating life. "Oh, look at that," Christine said. "You just pushed love away." It pissed me off because I knew she was right.

So, I started working on my attitude about dating. Things did not immediately get better but I kept trying to be positive. I went on a lot more dates. Nothing happened. Then, somewhere around the middle of the year, I got a message from Chris online asking me out to dinner. It was abrupt but I thought, "What the hell? That's what we are here for, right?" So, I agreed.

I'd already gotten a lemon drop martini from the bar when he ambled in, five minutes late. He was exactly my type. He ordered a rum and Coke and we began to casually review the first date stats. We are the exact same age. We've both been married twice. Neither of us have any children. Our black and white dogs look like matching bookends. He's a business owner, a risk taker, and he has mischievous gray-green eyes that light up when he's being silly. We even share a love of a cocktails.

There was no magical feeling or romantic music that night. To be honest, everything was pretty regular, but at the end of the night, I heard something in my brain click quietly, and I thought, "Does that mean something?"

I'm not going to tell you this is a storybook romance. We've fought and made up. I've had a dear friend of mine who has had an ongoing health scare. He's been through some excruciating pain from a crushed disk in his neck. There have been fights with coworkers, roommates and friends. One time we were even rear-ended on the way to a concert.

But there have also been unexpected moments like waiting in line together for the most famous BBQ in Phoenix, going to a

Simon & Garfunkel concert only to realize it was a tribute band, or riding bicycles through Old Town Scottsdale on a Sunday afternoon. Once, we stumbled upon an island in the middle of Lake Erie while we were in Ohio. He fell into the lake and I almost peed my pants laughing. If I live to be one hundred years old, I will always remember that day as one of the happiest days of my life.

So is this love? I'd like to think it is, yet I have no expectation on where it's going. I simply know I'm grateful for every moment I have with him. I know my life feels infinitely better with him than it does without him. He can be grumpy and a little rough around the edges but he also understands how to be kind. And instead of relying on me to be the dominating force to stir up trouble, he's a cyclone in his own right. Every night, we curl up together on the couch to watch the news, not because it is so informative but because that's where we decompress. And it fits a happy compartment of my life that has been empty for far too long.

Sometimes, I think of the woman I was a year ago, sitting up in my bedroom alone watching television feeling lonely and I know I'm a different person today. I opened my life to 52 new people looking to hear their stories and connect with them, but every time I walked away from someone new, I also took away a lesson. It made me better. It made me stronger. Our community really is a patchwork quilt. We can't become the people we are meant to be without each other. So why are we so afraid? The people we walk shoulder to shoulder with every day are actually pretty spectacular. None of my new friends were planned. They all just walked into my life.

And if I can randomly meet 52 amazing people like the ones immortalized in these pages, then what is your excuse?

Postscript

I thought I was done after I met my last new friend. I was feeling nostalgic and pretty good about myself, which is why I started to thinking back to the very first person I met on my 52 new friend's journey: Melissa.

I'd reached out to Melissa a few times over the last year but we could never seem to find the right time to connect face-to-face again. So, I sent her a text. We have been Facebook friends for a while now and I noticed something tragic had happened in her family. It seemed like her nephew had passed away. I didn't know if it was a car accident or if he'd been sick for a long time. He seemed very young. But like most people, I felt like it wasn't my place to ask.

When I sent Melissa the text, she told me her sixteen-year-old nephew had died by suicide. I was floored.

We met up for coffee a few days later and Melissa told me all about the bright, young man who was silly and loving and more than anything wanted to be a police officer. Melissa lives with Austin's mother, her sister. Austin's mother and father had been divorced for some time. One day at school, one of Austin's friends received a photo from a girl in her underwear. Although the photo hadn't been sent to him, he acted as any sixteen-year-old boy would. Austin looked at the photo. Some other kids told on the group of boys and they were suspended. For Austin, who had already been having feelings of depression, the suspension was more than he could bear. He must have feared he would never be a police officer and the next day, he took his own life.

I think Melissa had already cried all the tears she could. I cried more than she did. But here's the funny thing about life: Months before, I realized the blog I was writing needed to be a book. The idea for the project had come to me because I had stood at the American Foundation for Suicide Prevention's annual Out of the Darkness Walk the year before. I started this project because I wanted people in my community to know they were not alone. I had already decided that any proceeds from this book needed to go back to the American Foundation for Suicide Prevention. And all these months later, as I sat across from Melissa in a coffee shop, I knew this project could not have been started if it wasn't for her. It's like the evolution of this was planted before Austin's death, before I met Melissa, before I even knew it, myself. I did not plan for this project to come full circle…but it did.

So this book, 52 New Friends, is held in loving memory of Austin Hansen. He was a stand-up kid that just wanted to do what was right in the world. Maybe this book can, in some way, carry that spirit on. No one needs to feel as if they are unloved or alone. Austin's life mattered. So does yours.

Made in the USA
Middletown, DE
13 December 2019